LAND OF SKIES AND WATER

LAURENT FÉLIX-FAURE

Land of Skies and Water

Holland Seen Through the Eyes of Its Painters

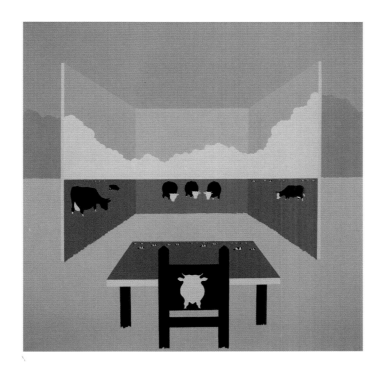

LEMNISCAAT ROTTERDAM

To my family.

Cover illustration: 'Cloud above Leeuwarden' by Douwe Elias
Title page illustration: 'Winter Landscape and Table' by Han Jansen
Book design: Maria van Donkelaar
Cover design: Gerolf T'Hooft
© Lemniscaat b.v. Rotterdam 1996
ISBN: 90 5637 059 6
Litho's: Litho-House, Rotterdam
Printed and bound in Belgium by Proost International Bookproduction, Turnhout

ACKNOWLEDGMENTS

First and foremost I would like to thank all the Dutch painters, living and dead, who have been a part of my life and have subsequently made their way into this book. They have taught me to look at Dutch landscapes differently and, more importantly, with a growing appreciation and respect. To this list I wish to add the Dutch poets included herein, at the same time asking them to pardon my poor attempts at translating their admirable works. It is unfortunate that the language barrier restricts their readership for, as in painting, Dutch poetry offers many rare and precious jewels. In the seventeenth century both art forms were regarded as being complementary to each other: painting was often alluded to as 'mute poetry', while poetry, as 'speaking painting'. Having used the one in my book, I naturally felt compelled to use some of the other!

I must confess to having been a veritable magpie in my use of books, catalogues and magazines, unashamedly culling the many interesting ideas of their authors. There are far too many excellent publications on the Netherlands and on Dutch art which make it impossible for me to form a comprehensive listing here – suffice it to say that these works have been a very useful source of information and I would not like them to go unmentioned.

Among the many persons who have helped me I feel particulary indebted to Hens de Jong, Arnold Niessen and Gerard Wensma. All three are extremely talented contemporary artists whose works appear in the book. Their generous advice when I embarked upon this venture proved invaluable. Leo van Heijningen, who is a professional painter as well as an art historian and a gallery owner, has been kind enough to screen the manuscript for facts. He also introduced me to a number of excellent artists. I wish to thank my friend, Dr Cees van Rhijn, for his interest and encouragement. As a psychiatrist and an art lover, he supported my 'subjective' approach which is based more on chance encounters, personal experience and insights, than on study and the analysis of data. Mary Zeilstra-Kroner helped me considerably when I wrote the original Dutch manuscript and Janey Tucker's sharp eye proved invaluable when I got down to the English version. Maud Schwab filed all the information on the artists and their work – no mean task – and has also, on many occasions, accompanied me when I visited artists at their studios. Our conversations on what we had seen and on art in general frequently helped to clarify my thoughts. Apart from my publishing house, Lemniscaat, which has followed all the stages of the project very closely, Maria van Donkelaar has done a remarkable job on the general presentation: her fine taste and sense of composition have benefitted the lay-out immensely and consequently the readabilty of the text.

The list of contributors would of course be incomplete without mentioning my family. They are a multi-cultural lot if ever there was one: my French father, my Dutch mother, my three children Jean-Laurent, Liesbeth and Karin who are both French and Dutch, my Dutch daughter-in-law, Caroline, who has sold her heart to Australia, my Ecuadorian son-in-law, Alejandro, and finally Anke, my wife, who is my whole world. Through them I have learnt to listen to many tongues and to see with many eyes. This book is an expression of my gratitude to them.

Laurent Félix-Faure, 18 August 1996

Very little remains today of the original Dutch landscape. This is perhaps just as well, for it must have been extremely dull: particularly impenetrable low woodlands stretched right across from the north to the south, while in the west, the sand dunes had free play. The Zuiderzee and the Waddenzee were yet to come into existence and the main rivers meandered freely to the south of the Veluwezoom.

The picturesque Dutch panorama that we are familiar with, was born out of the struggle between the primitive forces of nature and the diligence of the inhabitants of this little country. The first few centuries of our era were marked by angry attacks of the wind and water on the Dutch shores. The sea's fury smote gigantic holes in the landmass of areas around Zeeland and the Wadden, forcing the Flevo lake to burst its banks, turning it into the capricious Zuiderzee. Calm, gentle lakes swelled uncontrollably and metamorphosed into threatening inland seas as a result of the southwestern storms. This area with a relatively dense population – now known as North Holland – was soon depleted of its inhabitants as they fled in large numbers to higher, sandy reaches. Those who remained, withdrew to knolls which required frequent raising.

It was only in the late Middle Ages that the hitherto unconventional idea of actively resisting the elements was mooted by religious orders residing in monastries. Dikes were built, the low woodlands were raized to the ground and even the stumps were pulled out. Starting from the old cart tracks and the dike roads, ditches were dug so that long plots of meadowland came into existence. Farmers' dwellings were built along roads. After the first simple windmills had been constructed (appearing as strange, futuristic palings in the landscape!), it became possible to start reclamation, albeit on a small scale. What emerged was a landscape truly 'fashioned by hand'. While it is true that in de mid-nineteenth century much of it underwent a further change as a result of industrialisa-

tion and urbanisation, but broadly speaking the landscape retained the essential elements of its character.

A birds-eye view over Schiphol in clear weather will reveal the true beauty of a green countryside made up of fantastic natural shapes embedded in a landscape that was, once upon a time, 'reconstructed' using a measuring rod and a wheelbarrow.

To medieval man, the landscape was simply a narrow, enclosed piece of ground from which he had to eke out a living. With heaven above and hell below, and on the edge, the threatening sea – with its ominous underworld full of bizarre monsters – which ended over the horizon in a fathomless abyss where the foolhardy who dared go too far from home found their dreadful end, the landscape was thus restricted to not more than a day's journey for most people. Mobility was limited, only soldiers and seafarers and an odd artist travelled beyond the horizon. The great majority were tied to the city, glued to the ground of their birth, at the mercy of disease, war and the whims of nature.

The landscape was not an object of contemplation or admiration but merely a place of dwelling where one had been unceremoniously dumped for a short period to fight for life. The picture of the Dutch landscape is marked by these restrictions. It is the ideal scenery – the enclosed garden with flowers and plants, each with their own symbolism. It is the garden as depicted by the oriental world in its carpets: an idealized, almost unreal garden. It could also be the landscape where mankind wages its everyday struggle for existence: labouring farmers, lumberjacks, sowers and reapers, each with the underlying possibility of typifying the passing of the seasons, so often the case with illustrations in breviaries. The sea-scape, on the other hand, manages to include all the components of the threatening outside world, in all its chaos.

Towards the end of the Middle Ages and in the early Renaissance period, the landscape presented itself via vistas. From the seclusion of the rooms of prelates, wealthy persons and rulers, an over-the-shoulder glimpse at the world outside was presented. It seems as though they want to break out of the closeness of familiar surroundings.

The Renaissance turned the world of the simple mortal upside down. Nothing was clear cut or sacrosanct any more. Foundations were pulled away from under centuries' old certainties. The place of mankind itself was no longer clear, the hereafter uncertain. Those anxious in spirit cringed, the reckless ventured behind the curve of the horizon and carried on further, around the world. They conquered new continents and recorded them in the form of maps. These maps were not mere geographically delineated area lines such as what we might envisage; rather, they comprised of detailed sketches and notes written by the able helmsmen. These were reproduced as birds-eye views of far away foreign coasts, indicating not only suitable landing places but also pointing out the dangerous ones. They depicted sought after products and were, in short, illustrated journals of conquests.

The enthusiasm of the Renaissance artists knew no bounds. They seemingly performed magic with the recently discovered perspective and conjured up vistas on their canvas whereby the landscape was viewed as decorative for the first time. Artistic 'tricks' were made use of, an illustration of which we shall come across again later in the example of the laying out of parks and gardens in layers with a darker foreground and successively lighter ones behind, thereby evoking a strong suggestion of depth. The Calvinistic Dutch (with the exception of the Bentvogels who, throughout their lives, after their return from southern regions, painted landscapes in a plethora of unreal rich colours) attempted to show a divine plan in the Dutch landscape, in spite of the fact that their country had been shaped by human hands. In the belief that the need for organisation was decreed by God, they arranged perfect, glorious landscapes. Only the greats, such as Rembrandt van Rijn, saw the beauty of sheer 'chance'

and painted fragments of landscape which caught their artistic eye. In the seventeenth century, the Dutch 'Golden Age', tens if not hundreds of thousands of landscapes were painted. An oevre which, for the most part, originated in studios formed one great eulogy to creation. There were landscapes in which every object had its definite place, from the position of the sun to that of the clouds. There were landscapes also, that were dominated by the human presence: fishermen along the great rivers, the miller, the skaters on the frozen canals, the harvesting farmers. Nothing was left to chance.

Yet, interfering with nature was not enough. The need for organisation, categorisation and of classifying and thus controlling nature led, in particular in the eighteenth century, to remarkable interventions in the Dutch landscape. Wealthy people fled from the crowded cities and settled in the quiet countryside. In the landscape which had been worked upon by their forefathers, they created and demarcated their separate, organised plots of land. Small areas were enclosed by rectangular avenues of trees which shielded them from the wind. In the carving out of plots and vegetable and flower beds, a different landscape slowly emerged, much like an encyclopaedia wherein everything has its place and everything is explained. Contrarily enough, the self-imposed feeling of being stifled and boxed in was broken by using tricks of the perspective. Along the Vecht and Amstel rivers and in scores of other places, the landscape was cut up and altered like a patchwork quilt. The art of painting followed these very principles. Depictions of nature were narrowed down to concentrating on these miniature landscapes whereby the straightness of the ruler had gained dominance over the freedom of the brush. The landscape in the art of painting was reduced to pictures of the garden. On the face of it, as a violent reaction to the measured, straight lines of such depictions, Romanticism, wherever possible, replaced the unnatural geometric portrayals with a naturalness that is so intrinsic to nature.

Fanciful lines and unexpected vistas emerged in art. It is true that the straightness was broken but the planning and organisation were no less for it. The Netherlands have not exactly distinguished themselves in depicting romantic landscapes. Quite the contrary, in fact. While German Romanticism reached dramatic heights, with sentimental meadows and heavy masses of rock, and the English painters amused themselves in their Arcadia of splendid country estates, Dutch artists did not know how to create their own style but searched, together with poets and sculptors, for a safe refuge in a repeat of their Golden Age. An uninspired retouch, where they even went as far as to fill in nineteenth century paintings with seventeenth century figures and vehicles.

It was only under the influence of the French impressionism that they woke up and were enthused, and, like the Barbizon painters, placed their easels in the open fields. What they found there was the peacefulness of the nineteenth century landscape, stripped of every kind of drama, with lazy cows chewing their cud and quacking ducks under a willow tree. It is true that the sea could smash the flat bottomed boats to pieces, throwing them onto the beach every now and again, as the waves collided against the well-ordered dunes. The lakes were reduced to rippling waters where decoy-men and reed cutters were engaged in their craft. The large rivers dozed within their main dikes, here and there showing the possibility of discharging excess water at an overflow.

The only disorganised element was the weather: biting cold, a snowfall covering everything, days of threatening rain, sudden gusts of wind. Consequently, those of the Hague School as well as the Amsterdam impressionists represented the weather in particular: storm clouds, wet meadows, frozen canals, beaches bathed in a light drizzle.

In contrast to fellow artists from the sixteenth and seventeenth centuries, there was no question of a leaning towards being enticed by distances and far away locales. While French artists allowed themselves to be tempted by the colonies in a form of art which was validated under the name of orientalism, the Dutch stayed at home. It was not until after the First World War that a few hesitant artists were to travel to the Far East which led to the 'Beautiful Indonesian Style' that was to experience such an unexpected revival in the Eighties and Nineties.

The modern landscape, dominated by urbanisation and industrialisation, has merged with the rural landscape which was formed over a period of twenty centuries. The infrastructure crawls along old tracks. The landscape is caught within structures directed towards the future but determined ever since the Middle Ages. Primitive fear of the inconsistencies and vagaries of nature, and the need arising thereof to control the landscape, has turned full circle. A fear of a completely organised landscape and a need to let nature take its course, is being realised increasingly by allowing it free reign to run wild. It even takes on the bizarre extent of flooding reclaimed land so that the landscape shaped and ordered by human hands can be returned to the insecurity of the elements. The flow of twentieth century styles and trends in art has not bypassed Dutch landscape painters. The expressionists, cubists, surrealists and fauvists have bent the landscape to suit themselves so as to finish finally, in the last chapter of the twentieth century, in a sudden lean towards figuration whereby the landscape is given form so as to be experienced in a familiar yet different way.

With that, the circle is complete and the time has come to look back at the Dutch landscape as it is thought of, seen and imagined. The landscape can be seen and imagined by the painter and in turn, interpreted by the art historian, experienced by the inhabitants, put into words by the historian retrospectively, pondered on by the poet. It is the virtue of this book that all these aspects of experiencing the landscape have come together in a balanced manner. That this is being effected by an author who has walked around in the Dutch polders long enough to know what he is talking about but has remained enough of a Frenchman to let his spirit float above the landscape, has led to an original and refreshing look at the land of skies and water.

Ruud Spruit

Table of Contents

Introduction

There is a world of difference between looking at things with a sketch-book and pencil in hand and in just seeing them in the ordinary way. As a painter once said when talking about drawing the portrait of his girlfriend: 'I suddenly realised that what I thought I knew but I did not know at all: the nose of the girl I loved.'

Throughout the writing of this book, art has been the main reference point. Drawings and paintings by Dutch artists provide an invaluable insight into what might be termed the substance of the Dutch landscape. No one else, it would seem, is in a better position to provide an accurate picture of the country.

In this land of painters, the number of works of art is countless. Over the last five hundred years, Dutch painting has shown remarkable continuity. It has been said that 'Holland is the kindom of pictorial expression' and undoubtedly, Dutch culture owes a great deal to its painters. Even those who may not be able to locate Holland on a map of the world will know the names of Rembrandt, Vermeer, Van Gogh and Mondrian. A special blessing has apparently been bestowed upon the painters of this little country. And since, in keeping with tradition, these painted records are – for the greater part – based on matter-of-fact realism: they are easy to understand. Not only that, but they are also readily accessible. Thousands of books have been written about Dutch art and hundreds of museums all over Holland and abroad exhibit the work of Dutch artists. Consequently, anyone who chooses to, will discover a startling and unexpected treasure-trove. The works reproduced here will serve not only to illustrate the text, but, more importantly, to supplement it by highlighting particular aspects of the Dutch landscape as well as in disclosing some of the traits of its inhabitants.

Any selection from such a wealth of material will obviously be a matter of personal choice. The reproductions in this book and the interpretation of them therefore reflect the preferences and views of the author. But that is surely what artistic license is all about! Modern art bears witness to the fact that the model may be painted in red, green or yellow, it being unimportant whether the features have been slightly altered or not. As long as the portrait effectively conveys what it is meant to! Hopefully, once the last page has been turned, the author will feel free to echo the words of Max Lieberman: 'This painting, my dear Sir, resembles you more than you do yourself.'

Moreover, it should also be noted that the observations presented in the following pages are those of a foreigner. As an outsider to Dutch culture, he naturally approaches the canvas with a mind uncluttered with previous, familiar images. In that sense a parallel could be drawn with an artist who must empty his mind in order to effectively look at even the most well-known motif, as if for the very first time. Newness is often conducive to enthousiasm and enthousiasm in turn can be communicative. That is the spirit in which this book has been written

Painting as a Cultural Birth-Mark
The Dutch cultural philosopher, Ton Lemaire, suggests, that 'the landscape is the pictorial representa-

'If you ever come to Holland, I do hope you will recognise it from my paintings'

Jongkind

tion of a culture at a given moment in time: 'explicatio culturae', self-definition and self-representation of a culture.'

The contemporary art scene, particularly Western art, is subject to varied international trends: abstract expressionism, conceptual art, minimalism, hard-edged painting, pop art, photo-realism, etc. Under these circumstances, we may well ask ourselves whether it is still possible to speak of a specific Dutch art form and, if so, whether it can be considered a reliable source of information on Dutch culture. In this book, the assumption is in the affirmative.

Although today's shrinking world has certainly resulted in a greater degree of interaction between peoples than ever before, artists in the past were in fact quite used to travelling to visit their colleagues abroad. They also shared experiences with each other and mutual influence was widespread. Many seventeenth century Dutch painters went to Italy as a matter of course to perfect their art. Later, in the eighteenth and early nineteenth centuries, English landscape artists were indebted to the seventeenth century Dutch painters, whom they greatly admired and they, in turn, were a source of inspiration to the French outdoor painters of Barbizon. It is a well established fact that these French artists largely contributed to the revival of Dutch landscape painting of the members of the Hague School.

However, none of these influences ever led to any loss of identity. Johan Barthold Jongkind, who worked in France for the greater part of his life and set a lasting example to French impressionism, wrote to a friend in 1856: 'If you ever come to Holland, I do hope that you will recognise it from my paintings. And the landscapes are beautiful because they possess a national spirit, I say national, for everything here speaks of a Dutch nationality, such as, I believe, you will not find elsewhere.' Technological developments have, without doubt, brought about a degree of uniformity in certain geographical areas. The surroundings in which artists grow up look more and more alike. However, Holland is not France and Spain is not Norway. Some years ago when the Centre Pompidou in Paris organised an international exhibition of twentieth century art under the title 'Les realismes', the differences were obvious: the infallible sense of form of the Italians, the tendency of German artists to exaggerate effects, an English inclination towards slightly seamy and melancholic scenes and the Dutch love of carefully worked-out and well-integrated detail. The contrasts are striking when Stanley Spencer from England is compared with Otto Dix from Germany, or the Italian Morandi with the Dutchman Dick Ket. The exhibition could not have hoped for a more convincing demonstration of cultural identities. Referring to the past, a well-known art historian, Elie Faure, once wrote: 'Obviously, around 1650, every Dutchman was not a Rembrandt, every Spaniard not a Velasquez, every Frenchman not a Poussin. But, knowing the first to be a Dutchman, the second a Spaniard and the third a Frenchman, it is easier to understand why they painted as they did.'

Michiel Kranendonk (1966), The Lek at Culemborg, colour woodcut, 1993, 16.5 x 43 cm.

Holland Seen Through the Eyes of Its Painters

When I think of Holland
I see winding rivers
Making their way
Across endless plains,
Rows of Poplars
So unbelievably slight
Standing against the horizon...

H. Marsman

'When I Think of Holland...'

'When I think of Holland...' what kind of landscape springs immediately to mind? Grassy lowlands with grazing cattle, vast skies and impressive clouds reflected in the waters of lakes and canals. Does such a landscape really exist or is it merely a figment of the imagination? An oft painted, classic representation of a Dutch landscape, which may well have disappeared since, might, out of habit, continue to be painted by future generations of artists. While much has changed, it is true, classic Dutch scenery has not altogether ceased to exist, at least in large parts of the coastal provinces.

To begin with, it would be a mistake to believe that the Dutch landscape consists exclusively of the much publicized marshy polders in the reclaimed areas of the country. Beyond the polders that lie below sea-level, the countryside takes on other aspects. Of course, in comparison with neighbouring countries, the wooded hills of Overijssel, Gelderland and Utrecht are mere bumps and hollows, modest moraines left behind by the glaciers that once covered this part of Europe. But they do possess a special charm, and often it is quite 'un-Dutch'. Down south, the beautiful, rolling countryside of Limburg has some fairly deep valleys through which the Meuse winds its way. Painters from these friendly surroundings often use a brightly coloured palette containing a hint of the stained-glass windows of their catholic churches. Then there is Brabant, which is quite different again, where Vincent van Gogh was born and made his early, earthy paintings. The delta regions of the great rivers and the coastal provinces on which we focus in this book are completely different; there is no place on earth that resembles them at all closely. They present an extraordinary and fascinating amalgam of semi-natural and artificial landscapes – some of them created wholly by man. The humid climate and the distant views in these parts of the Netherlands offer an incredible array of changing colours and tonal values which landscape artists never tire of painting. Seascapes, beaches and dunes, polders neatly sliced up by canals and ditches, lakes and rivers: they are all there, crammed together in this little country. And to crown the lot, there is that wide open and ever-changing sky, generously dispensing golden and silvery light and every imaginable shade of grey. It is hardly surprising that Dutch painting began here, or that Dutch painters were such early exponents of the art of landscape painting.

Maike van de Kooy (1951), Countryside near Zuidwolde – Groningen, acrylic on canvas, 1994, 200 x 52 cm.

Over recent decades the physical appearance of this landscape has changed, in some instances very radically. Half a century ago, the province of Zeeland was still largely insular and the first polders in the IJsselmeer were just vast mudflats. It should be noted that the term landscape is derived from the old Dutch 'landskip' (modern Dutch 'landschap'). Etymologically the syllable 'schep/schap' in Dutch refers to the act of creating and nothing could be truer so far as the Dutch landscape is concerned. Holland is unique in the sense that pure, unadulterated nature simply does not exist, anywhere within its national boarders. Every single bit of the country has been conceived by the human mind. Behind every tree, flower and blade of grass there lies an idea. In the province of South-Holland alone, 30,000 kilometers of ditches have been dug

– enough to stretch all the way from Amsterdam to Sydney and a good part of the way back. The Dutch are perpetually shaping and reshaping their country: in the past, to reclaim land for agricultural purposes, in more recent times, to recreate nature in order to palliate the adverse effects of urbanisation. In some areas canals are even being remodelled into romantic and sparkling brooks that pass through shady groves of carefully selected saplings. No wonder it has been said that these days Holland paints its landscapes with bulldozers!

Inside every Dutchman there lurks an architect, a planner, a construction-worker just trying to get out. A passing peep into their homes between the permanently drawn back curtains suffices to justify this statement. In each and every living-room a landscape has been lovingly recreated. Vases of fa-

miliar flowers and pots containing exotic plants line the window-sill, half-grown trees stand next to armchairs and dusting around the cacti requires special skills only acquired through long and diligent practice.

This continuous refurbishing of personal habitat – indoors and out – is indubitably a source of satisfaction to the Dutch. In his book, 'The Embarrassment of Riches', the historian Simon Schama quotes on this point the sixteenth-century hydraulic engineer Andries Vierlingh: 'The making of new land belongs to God alone for he gives to some people the wit and the strength to do it.' An elegant formulation which combines the Christian virtues of modesty and humility to which the Dutch are profoundly attached, with a certain propensity to occasional self-satisfaction.

The pace at which these changes occurr in the Dutch landscape, with space becoming scarcer and demographic pressures growing, prompted Hens de Jong to make her painting 'Trucks in Evening Landscape': buildings rush by as the vehicles speed down concrete highways with only a few patches of green polderland left on either side.

Wendelien Schönfeld clearly shares the same concern.

Hans Bogaarts shows how very much out of place new buildings can look. A lonely edifice sticking out like a sore thumb right in the middle of an empty polder is also a familiar sight. After all, the country is so flat that every single building or structure stands out and is visible from a great distance.

But there are also remarkable achievements of great beauty. The spectacular and uncluttered urban development is one of them. A city with a port of gigantic proportions like of Rotterdam, with its wide open waterways and modern skyline has none of the grubbiness of the usual harbour; it looks as if it has just been washed and polished.

A closely knit network of highways covers the whole country – broad motorways that roll out neatly over a tidy countryside in which electric trains dart hither and thither like tiny mechanical yellow lizards. Even the modern multi-story buildings of glass and steel on the skyline fail to look awesome: the sky is far too high for them to appear oversized and Dutch urban planning far too measured to allow uncontrolled development. It is really quite amazing how the rural and urban landscapes lock together and blend, even if at times the price is uniformity. This particular concept of space and the Dutch talent for using it to optimal effect has ensured the preservation of much of the beauty of the country in spite of demographic pressures and industrial and urban development. There is still more than enough left for people to enjoy and for future generations of artists to paint.

Page 16: Wendelien Schönfeld (1950), Landscape 1, oil on canvas, 1984, 80 x 105 cm.

Top: Hens de Jong (1929), Trucks in Evening Landscape, oil, 1985, 140 x 120 cm.

Bottom: Hans Bogaarts (1948), Three Polder Landscapes, oil on canvas, 1981, 30 x 450 cm; 30 x 20 cm.; 30 x 40 cm.

Basic Elements of the Dutch Landscape

The classic Dutch landscape comprises a number of basic elements. There is usually a long horizontal line cutting the picture in two (the horizon), intersected by one or more vertical lines (a windmill, church tower or some other kind of building) and two or three diagonal lines (a receding ditch, canal, dike or row of trees) converging to a vanishing point just above the horizon.

The 'Schilderboeck' (The Painter's Book) by Carel van Mander, published in 1604, is not an easy read, since it is in verse and the language is archaic. The book was written to help artists by giving them tips on how to paint Dutch landscapes but, by the same token, it draws attention to various characteristics of the landscape. For example, Van Mander points out how ditches and furrows in the field taper and converge to the same vanishing point, just like a tiled floor. 'I want you to draw attention to the

kind of foreshortening and reduction that you see in nature. Although it is not architecture for which you need to follow precise rules, you still need to fix your focal point on the horizon ... Everything below that line will appear as if seen from above, while everything else will appear as if seen from below.'

A few examples drawn from the treasure-trove of Dutch painting will help show how consistently this methodical approach has been used – consciously or otherwise – in landscape painting ever since. It makes no difference whether the painter is Esaias van de Velde in the early seventeenth century, Weissenbruch in the nineteenth or Douwe Elias today: all three use the simple formula of a horizontal dividing line and vertical and converging lines, although obviously, from a purely artistic point of view, their works continue to bear the stamp of their authors.

Esaias van de Velde (1591-1630), The Cattle Ferry, oil, 1622, 75.5 x 113 cm.

Jan Hendrik Weissenbruch (1824-1903), View of the Trekvliet near The Hague, oil on canvas, 1870, 65 x 100 cm.

Douwe Elias (1952), Cloud above Leeuwarden, oil on canvas, 1995, 110 x 160 cm.

This beautiful watercolour by Arnold Niessen is based on the same schema. Interestingly, although it is a realistic work, the 'T' form on the wharf in the foreground of the view of the lake, is perhaps a subconscious reference to Mondrian.

There is bound to be some sort of relationship between the geometrical lay-out of the polder landscape and the vertical and horizontal planes of the abstract works painted by Mondrian, one of the most significant artists of the twentieth century. Author and art historian Joop Joosten, who has devoted most of his life to the study of Mondrian's work, does not, for one moment, doubt that there is: 'Mondrian found a way to work in line and colour and to paint the essence of art – that is Dutch art – based on horizontal and vertical lines.'

There is a nice story that provides a significant illustration of the way this reduction of a landscape to lines continued to obsess Mondrian even when he was abroad. During a train journey through the lush French countryside, he looked out of the window and was overheard muttering under his breath: 'Isn't it wonderful to see them go by, continually cutting the horizon, here and here and here.' He was admiring the telegraph poles.

At first sight, Mondrian's 'Composition 10; Pier and Ocean' looks nothing at all like the subject it is supposed to represent. Can this really be a painting of curling waves and the undulating surface of the sea? Yet a closer scrutiny clearly reveals that this criss-cross pattern of short horizontals and verticals is a faithful and convincing rendition of the subject it is supposed to represent. Undeniably, a remarkable achievement of reduction to what one observer, the art critic Robert Hughs, has termed 'a divided field of twinkling intersections'.

'A landscape reduced to vertical and horizontal lines'

Page 20: Arnold Niessen (1947), The Reeuwijk Lakes, watercolour, 1982, 35 x 47.5 cm.

Piet Mondrian (1872-1944), Composition 10; Pier and Ocean, oil on canvas, 1915, 85 x 108 cm.

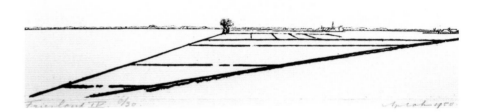

Left: Fon Klement (1930), A Landscape in Friesland, oil on canvas, 1985, 30 x 30 cm.

Right: Ap Sok (1917), Friesland IV, etching, 1950, 21.3 x 30.2 cm.

'Back to the basic scheme'

The fact that a Dutch landscape can be reduced to horizontal and vertical lines also implies, according to Joop Joosten, that 'Dutch art is two-dimensional. It has depth but all movements run parallel to the picture plane. Look at a seventeenth century seascape and the boats in it. They are all drawn parallel, or practically parallel, to the picture plane. You can wander around in a Rubens landscape. It continues beyond the horizon.' In Dutch paintings, on the contrary, the landscape is a wide, unbroken surface and the taut delineation of a remote horizon creates the illusion of a boundary.

The geometrical approach to the Dutch landscape led Fon Klement to simplify 'A Landscape in Friesland' to the extreme. As for Ap Sok, when he made 'Friesland IV' he simply drew the basic scheme, consisting of a single horizontal line and two diagonal lines.

Seascapes are very much the natural extension of the flat rolled out Dutch landscape. The distant horizon also makes them seem limited, a fact that used to worry early navigators and explorers who believed there was a chance they might sail right over the brink. All that needs to be done to make a picture is to add one or two vertical lines cutting the horizon, a lighthouse for instance or the mast of a ship. The white sail is cut out against a cloudy sky in a seventeenth century painting 'Agitated Sea' by Jacob van Ruisdael.

What holds true for the land and seascapes, ceases to apply to the vast skies above the horizon. They are usually magnificently adorned with impressive clouds, the sculptured forms of which provide the plasticity lacking in the country beneath. The light that shines through these masses of condensed vapour has a particularly rich quality which has been one of the trade marks of Dutch painting ever since it began. In essence, therefore, the Dutch landscape has two highly distinct and opposing faces rolled into one. There is the flat, gridded land kept orderly and under close control by its inhabitants. Above it, separated by the dividing line of the horizon, there is a vast and changeable sky governed by unpredictable moods. This tension between a rationally organised country and an unpredictable sky is specific to the Dutch landscape and may explain some of the appeal it continues to hold for painters.

Studies have been made on the perceptual reactions to horizontal-vertical stimuli on persons from industrialised and non-industrialised cultures. Those who are unfamiliar with rectangular buildings apparently experience difficulty, for example, in assessing the lengths of horizontals and verticals in relation to one another. A not altogether unlikely side-effect of the strictly geometrical patterns of the Dutch landscape is the way it may influence the perceptual judgments of its inhabitants; measuring and evaluating have become part and parcel of the Dutch mental make up and they are famous for it.

Place the blue of the sea
against the blue of the sky
brush in a slash of white for a sail
and the wind will rise.

Willem Hussem

Jacob van Ruisdael (1628/29-1682), Agitated Sea, oil on canvas, ca. 1670, 107 x 124.5 cm.

Sky and Light: the Great Magicians

Kees van Roemburg (1914), Near Avenhorn, gouache, 1986

According to Carel Mander, the author of the 'Schilderboeck', Dutch paintings have sometimes been criticised by foreigners for their grey, cloudy skies. Using mythological references to make their point, they complain that Apollo in his quality of sun god hardly ever got the chance to peep down through a hole in the sky at the earth. More recently, Picasso said that it was always half night in Holland. He could just as well have said half day, which is closer to the truth. And he could also have added that the infinite gradations of light which the skies of Holland so generously dispense are a painter's dream come true.

Dutch skies are forever changing. There is rarely a dull moment as a richly costumed parade of clouds slowly makes its way across the monumental stage. Sometimes they are jumbled and panicky, at other times slow and stately; there is no end to the shapes they choose to take.

The writer, Maarten 't Hart, narrates how a painter he admires, Kees van Roemburg, often includes pointed clouds in his Dutch landscapes. 'Clouds like those don't exist,' he thought when he saw them for the first time. But, 'not three days later, I saw that type of cloud above the rooftops and ever since then I see them frequently. I now call them Van Roemburg clouds.'

Looking at clouds through a window can be a bit like standing in front of a framed painting. They can be whimsical and even pull a curtain over the carefully plotted landscape. Sometimes they are no more than the merest brush-stroke against a clear blue background. But Holland would not be so if they did not frequently, fill the sky with their heavy masses. Alex Verduyn has turned the clouds into huge cauliflowers whereas Karel Appel has painted them black over the city.

Top: Alexander Verduyn den Boer (1958), Clouds, oil on canvas, 1990, 100 x 130 cm.

Bottom: Karel Appel (1921), Black Clouds above a Town, oil on canvas, 1984, 203 x 345 cm.

Hens de Jong (1929), Blue Cloud above the North Sea, oil, 1990, 130 x 170 cm.

Page 27, top: Hans Gritter (1942), The Wadden Sea, watercolour, 1984, 13 x 20 cm.

Page 27, bottom: Piet Mondrian (1872-1944), The Red Cloud, oil, 1907, 64 x 75 cm.

Clouds have their moods. They can smile and look angry and pull the funniest faces. The greatest actor would find it hard to imitate them. They can change into people and animals, into mountains and buildings.

Hans Gritter has retained the perceptions of a child and there are figures in the clouds in his watercolour. Even Jan Klaassen (the main character in the Dutch Punch and Judy show) seems to be floating in the air and pointing a finger at the world below.

Anyone inclined to believe that clouds are white should take another look. When it was exhibited for the first time, Mondrian's 'Red Cloud' was a novelty

Hens de Jong's 'Blue Cloud above the North Sea' is beautiful but these days nobody will be surprised to see a blue cloud like the one she painted.

I wore my little clothes and lay
Beside mother in the warm sun.
Above us the clouds drove by.
And mother asked what I saw in them.
And I called out: 'Scandinavia!' and 'A fir-tree'
'Look there goes a lady! Sheep and a shepherd!'

Martinus Nijhoff

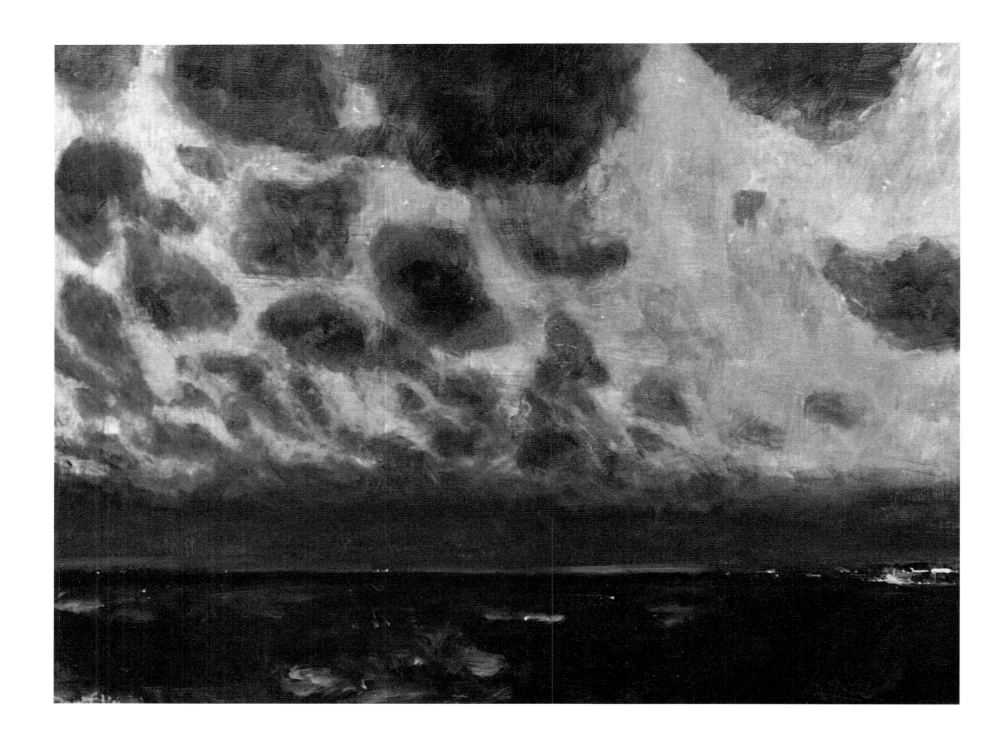

'Clouds tumbling down'

Driving home late one evening, Douwe Elias was struck by the sight of clouds apparently tumbling out of the sky like rocks. He couldn't wait to make a painting of what he had just witnessed: a moonlit sky and enormous chunks of cloud descending like meteors onto the low horizon of the Friesland polders. The far-away glow of a petrol station emphasizes the feeling of alienation in this curious night scene. Two other painters from Friesland had been looking at clouds before him: Gerrit Benner and Boele Bregman, both self-taught artists of exceptional talent. In Benner's painting, the sky and the land merge and a few drawn-out horizontal strokes of white, blue and yellow paint are sufficient to catch the essence of the landscape. Although at first this may look like an abstract painting, it isn't really. It is a landscape seen through half closed eyes. Details fall away and colours are filtered by the eyelashes so that only broad bright patches remain.

Boele Bregman's paintings are an altogether different proposition: his sky is interiorised, mysterious and even slightly mystical. The people of Friesland are said to conceal a passionate nature behind their public reserve. They have produced revolutionary statesmen and they love their Frisian language as only romantics can, for whom the poetry of the past is also a meaningful part of the present.

Page 28: Douwe Elias (1952), Frisian Landscape with Petrol Station, oil, 1991, 110 x 160 cm.

Top: Gerrit Benner (1897-1981), Skies and Water, oil, ca. 1970, 86 x 100 cm.

Bottom: Boele Bregman (1918-1980), Landscape with Clouds, oil on canvas, 1965, 100 x 120 cm.

Jan Hendrik Weissenbruch (1824-1903), View of Haarlem, detail, oil on panel, undated, 23.5 x 34 cm.

Page 31: Jacob van Ruisdael (1628/29-1682), Bleaching Fields near Haarlem, oil on canvas, 1670, 43 x 38 cm.

'Painters can never spend enough time looking at the sky'

The Mauritshuis museum in The Hague possesses 'Bleaching Fields near Haarlem' by Jacob van Ruisdael. He made several such views from the same vantage point, known collectively – with the Dutch diminutive 'tje' – as his 'Haarlemtjes'. Within a picture plane no larger than 43 x 38 cm, the artist has epitomized the beauty of the Dutch landscape. The plain is viewed from the top of a dune. It is bathed in light and shade. Billowing clouds drift across the sky.

Like most of his countrymen at the time Ruisdael was a firm believer. Art historians will point out that as a result of the Reformation, seventeenth century artists living and working in the Northern Netherlands had been deprived of traditional Catholic Christian imagery such as annunciations, nativities or crucifixions with which to express their religious impulses and many of them, like Ruisdael, channelled these feelings into their landscapes: 'His love for the magnificence of the creation of God is innate and spontaneous'. It is likely that the natural beauty of the sky aroused in Ruisdael a sense of divine awe and reverence. An indication may be in the very size given to the church of St Bavo on the horizon; it clearly stands out and is obviously much larger than it would have been on a normal scale. Nevertheless, in this landscape by Ruisdael, it is dwarfed to nothingness by the vastness of God's celestial kingdom!

Two centuries later, Jan Hendrik Weissenbruch – one of the main figures of the Hague School – spent a long time studying the Ruisdael painting and was even inspired by it to produce his own remarkable 'View of Haarlem'. He too was a master at rendering skies. 'The sky in a painting, that is something; that is what it is all about. Sky and light – they are the great magicians. The sky determines the whole painting. Painters can never spend enough time looking at the sky,' he is claimed to have said.

Gerard Wensma's work is a good example of the continuation of the great Dutch tradition of painting still-lives: the sheer unparalleled and personal joy of putting together a few familiar objects and reproducing them. Here, the impact of the still-life is heightened by a background of reverie. The artist seems to have paused from time to time to gaze through the window of his studio at the clouds.

Another painter of clouds, Jan Voerman, lived and worked in the area around the River IJssel during the early part of the present century. He never tired of looking at the cloud formations above the river – in the early morning and at dusk, in warm weather and during the winter. In fact, he went so far as actually to identify with the clouds. 'Do you know,' he once said to a friend, 'the clouds you see in my paintings are not really as they are, but me as I am inside!'

The clouds in Jentsje Popma's 'Colza Fields in the Lauwersmeerpolder' look like masonry in the sky, as though the artist wished to make quite sure they would stay where they were. Could it be a projection of his feelings? The artist had become so concerned about what would happen to the Dutch landscape if nothing were done to protect it that he put aside his sculptor's hammer and chisel in order to paint. He felt that it was urgent to record as many landscapes as possible before they disappeared forever.

Painters apparently are not overly concerned with whether those painted skies full of clouds actually corresponded to the season or the type of weather in the painting. The main purpose of a cumulus or a cirrus in the skies of a seventeenth century painting seems to be either to give consistency to the composition or to create the proper mood. In that respect, they are an extremely useful prop. And there is no stage lighting in the world that can so rapidly change angles, sharply focus a beam of light or provide such delicately diffused illumination. The clouds are the great regulators of this ongoing and impressive spectacle.

'The clouds you see in my paintings are not really as they are, but me as I am inside'

Page 32, top: Gerard Wensma (1919), Looking outside, oil, 1965, 120 x 90 cm.

Page 32, bottom: Jan Voerman (1857-1941), Cattle on the Banks of the IJssel, watercolour, undated, 63 x 82.5 cm.

Jentsje Popma (1921), Colza in the Lauwersmeerpolder, oil on panel, 1988, 38 x 46 cm.

Distant Horizons

Han Jansen (1931-1994), *Winter Landscape and Table*, oil on canvas, 1970, 100 x 100 cm.

A nation that has built a good part of its own landscape by reference to a ruler and geometrical formulas has little use for intuition and improvisation. The ideal is that everything should be planned in advance. The old adage, 'Deus Mare, Batavus litora fecit!' (God created the sea and the Dutch created their coastline), has been illustrated with humour by Han Jansen. It might, of course, be interesting to speculate on what would have happened if God had been a Dutchman! Sitting at his drawing-board, would He have divided the earth into neat little rectangular plots?

The broad prospect continuing uninterrupted to the horizon is an important feature in Dutch landscapes. Painters from mountainous areas may appreciate the existence of a horizon, but they do not constantly see it. There is a theory that being in this way cut off from a horizon has tended to make them curious and fire their imaginations, while the inhabitants of the plains don't need to speculate about what might be on the other side of a hill or a mountain and are therefore more down to earth. It is certainly true that imagination as such is not particularly important to the Dutch. This was recently confirmed by a survey carried out by a number of European publishers of popular romantic fiction. They were curious about the kind of man their largely female readership regarded as ideal in real life. What emerged was that Dutch women, in particular, showed very little interest in the creative and imaginative type of man. No artists, musicians or even scientists for them, but a businessman. As many as nineteen per cent dreamt of a magnate in industry. The Dutch are realists and their painting bears the stamp of realism. There are very few elves living in Holland, and certainly no trolls!

The wide open landscape with views limited only by the horizon might also explain why Holland became a land of painters. This has been suggested by Demetrius Boulger in his book 'Holland of the Dutch': 'In the absence of anything sensational and remarkable, attention is automatically drawn to details and their perfect harmony creates a new ideal of beauty. Something of this feeling has certainly permeated the mind of the Dutch. Painting is in the blood of these people to a greater degree than in any other country of Europe.'

The beautiful wash drawing by Jan van Spronsen is a good example of a wide open Dutch landscape. Two parallel horizontal lines – a dike and the horizon – divide the space and that is all the artist needs to compose his picture.

Jan van Spronsen (1932), Zuiderzee Works, wash drawing, 1966, 43 x 26.5 cm.

'Sky and earth: ideal and reality merge here'

Rembrandt van Rijn (1606-1669), The Three Trees, etching with dry-point, 1643, 21.1 x 28 cm.

Foreigners like the French writer Paul Claudel have often become quite lyrical when writing about the apparently never-ending expanses of the polder landscape: 'Here, in this landscape, it is as though one were the inhabitant or the guest of a vast, green, liquid plain on which the eye travels so quickly that the foot loses all desire to walk.' To which Henri Asselin, a foreign journalist, does not hesitate to add, 'sky and earth, ideal and reality merge here, and this holds rare poetry in it.'

The horizon, according to this principle, acts as a dividing line between two levels of perception: the image formed on the retina and those resulting from the stirrings of the soul.

Rembrandt knew, long before Sigmund Freud, that

the unruffled surface of the ideal conceals another reality. With one of his best-known etchings 'The Three Trees' he achieves a striking contrast (they are, in fact, a reminder of the three crosses on Cavalry in the Bible: 'Now from the sixth hour there was darkness over all the land unto the ninth hour'(Matthew 27:45). Above the line of the horizon, the restless sky casts light and shadow on the earth beneath. At the foot of the dune on which the three trees stand, however, there is a pretty little lake. A man is fishing and beside him is a woman. Nearly hidden by the brush, two lovers embrace. There are many other details in this etching that speak of peace and calm: fields, woods, mills, a horse pulling a carriage full of travellers and the outline of a city, Amsterdam, in the distance; there is even an artist sketching on the hill. Nobody seems to be aware of what is going on in the sky.

The drawing by Hendrik Goltzius is much less dramatic. It was probably made during one of the walks the artist took around 1600 in the Kennermerland for reasons of health (he is known to have suffered from consumption). The sketch is a straightforward and sensitive study of these familiar surroundings. The sky and earth occupy equal space. The tenuous line of the horizon is made slightly ragged by the intrusion of rooftops, a row of trees and, inevitably, church spires. This drawing and a few others are regarded by art historians as milestones in the evolution of seventeenth century landscape art. Goltzius was the first to show an awareness of the purely Dutch character of the landscape he recorded, in particular that it was a country reclaimed from the sea. He took care to note the dunes, the neatly laid out fields, the farmsteads nestling in clumps of trees and the distant horizon.

In the sketch by Jan van Goyen, the same wispy horizon can be seen, with the same irregularities where there are trees and roofs, mills and a church spire. This time, however, the artist is looking over a stretch of water.

Top: Jan van Goyen (1596-1656), View of a River with Ships, drawing, black chalk, Indian ink wash, 1650-1651, 9.9 x 15.7 cm.

Bottom: Hendrick Goltzius (1558-1617), Dutch panoramic Landscape, pen drawing, 1603, 7.8 x 19.7 cm.

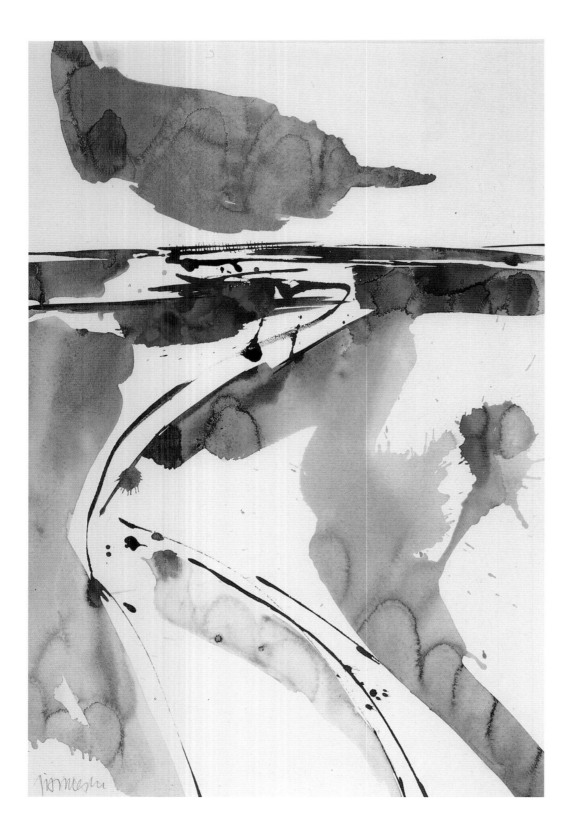

The horizon can also be viewed from an unusual angle. Johan Meeske has placed it high up in his composition. There is hardly any transition between land and sky. Only a few horizontal brush strokes divide them. The watercolour could easily be turned upside down and seen as an abstract version of the classical Dutch landscape with its low horizon and towering skies.

Another contemporary artist, Sjoerd de Vries, has also adopted the high horizon variant. His style, however, is very different. There is a strong degree of identification with his surroundings: the flat polder landscape running up to a distant horizon. 'From the time I was very young I could remember things I saw very clearly. Really sharply... my mother's kitchen window... she always stood at the sink. Then I looked out of the window at the polders that stretched out over a distance of twelve kilometers.' Interestingly, rather than using the conventional perspective lines converging to the horizon, Sjoerd de Vries conveys a sense of space through an accumulation of ellipses and rectangles.

Johan Meeske (1950), Landscape, watercolour, 1995, 70 x 90 cm.

'A different sense of space'

Sjoerd de Vries (1941), Landscape, mixed media on cardboard, 1977, 52 x 30 cm.

Artists will often choose to make their sketches from the top of a dune or a hill in order to obtain a better view. In the seventeenth century, Jacob van Ruisdael stood on a dune near the city to study the area for his famous 'Haarlempjes'. Today, Douwe Elias takes no half measures. He climbed to the very top of an eighty-metre tower under construction overlooking Leeuwarden, the capital of the province of Friesland. The result is a breathtaking panoramic view of the east side of the city and the horizon beyond.

'From an unusual point of view'

Douwe Elias (1952), View of Leeuwarden-East, oil on canvas, 1994, 200 x 200 cm.

Hermanus Berserik rose to even greater heights. He once wrote that the Dutch landscape was as flat as a billiard table. 'When I am drawing outdoors, I feel more and more inclined to draw across both pages of my sketch-book. I use the sort of sketch-book with a coiled spring back less and less frequently because they have become a nuisance.' As a background to his 'Self-portrait above the Polder', he has chosen the sky. The view that the artist has imagined is the one shared by seagulls and air travellers about to land or who have just taken off from Schiphol airport.

Hermanus Berserik (1921), Self-portrait above the Polder, oil on canvas, 1973, 100 x 110 cm.

The horizon not only serves as a dividing line, but is sometimes used by modern Dutch artists to break routine or as a playful element in their rendering of landscape.

Co Westerik is undoubtedly one of the most significant contemporary Dutch artists. 'The Wrist' represents an arm stretched out just above the horizon. The wrist is disintegrating and flaky fragments are floating in the air like clouds.

Ger van Elk has taken an altogether different look at the horizon. In his painting 'Dutch Grey', the line of the horizon divides the canvas in two equal parts, whereas the sides of the frame seem to represent the converging lines normally used in the picture to convey a sense of perspective.

Ger van Elk (1941), Dutch Grey, pencil and acrylic, 1984, 24.7 x 49.7 cm.

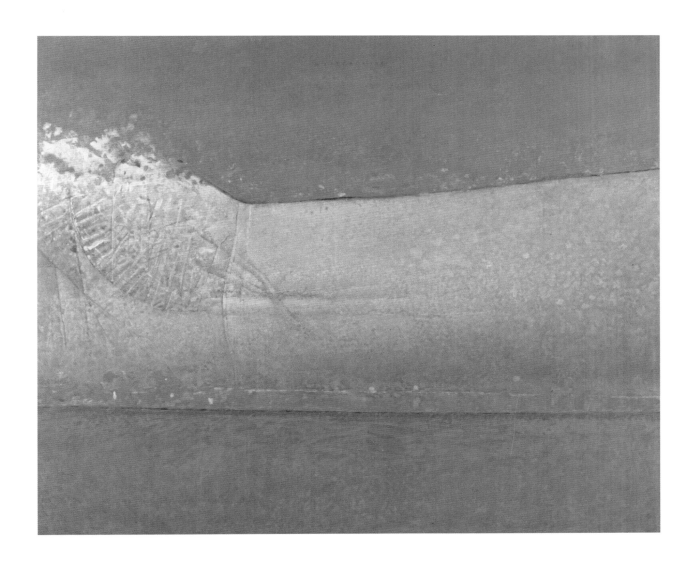

Co Westerik (1924), The Wrist, oil and tempera on canvas, 1981, 87 x 106 cm.

'Symmetry'

Ben Akkerman (1920), Row of Trees, oil on canvas, 1971/72, 43.5 x 43.5 cm.

Meindert Hobbema (1638-1709), The Avenue at Middelharnis, oil on canvas, 1689, 103.5 x 141 cm.

Ben Akkerman has opted for symmetry in his illustration of the Dutch landscape. The curved lines of a cumulus cloud are repeated in the foreground, possibly representing their reflection in water. The very subtle use of green and blue makes for variation and balance, as do the rounded treetops. This interpretation of the Dutch landscape looks modern but is not altogether new.

The well-known 'Avenue at Middelharnis' by Meindert Hobbema was painted three hundred years ago and the resemblance to Akkerman's work is striking.

Finally, there is a surprising horizon which opens like a fan, painted by the conceptual artist Jan Dibbets. He seems to have looked at his subject through a wide-angle lens. The horizon is no longer the familiar straight line. In 'Universe / A construction' the artist has over-emphasized reality – which is the curving line of the horizon around the globe – to achieve what he has termed, 'corrected perspective'.

'Corrected perspective'

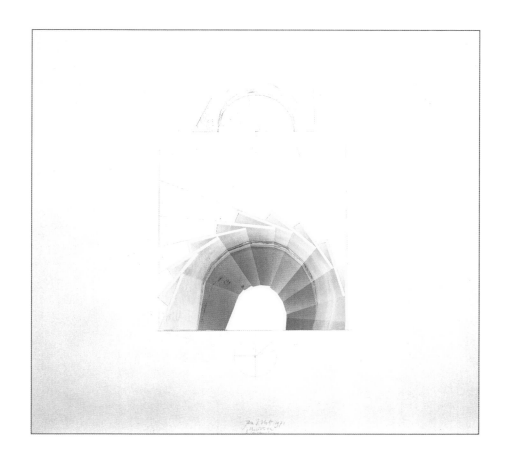

Jan Dibbets (1941), Universe / A Construction, colour prints, pencil, paper, 1971, 65 x 70 cm.

The Sea: Friend or Foe?

Sometimes you let me stand alone by tides high and low.
Hours go by tracing letters in the sand.
I resist, shrieking birds circling in the air above,
transient, outcast on the edge of the earth.
The waters come and go, the beach is shiny wet and empty as before.

Ida Gerhardt

Long ago, there was no clear border line between the land and the sea. Between 15000 and 5000 years B.C., a vast lagoon formed behind the coastal dunes, fed by the waters of the rivers. Mudflats appeared on the surface and a swampy archipelago developed which must have given the landscape a protoplasmic aspect. The crumbling barrier of the dunes was insufficient to keep the sea from breaking through and the tides invaded large areas of land before receding again.

Pytheas, a man from the Greek colony Marseille, who sailed along the coast of Holland around 325 B.C., was so impressed by this phenomenon that he gave an account of how 'the lungs of the sea regularly rose up and went down.' And, when raging storms struck the coast, as they regularly did, they caused widespread flooding.

Stella van Acker considered Ida Gerhardt's poem as particularly suited to her watercolour 'Sea'. 'Poetry is extremely important and I always read some before I go out to paint,' she says. On her home island of Schiermonnikoog in the Waddenzee, Stella van Acker still experiences something of the timelessness of nature and it permeates her work.

Hendrik Willem Mesdag (1831-1915), The North Sea, oil on canvas, 1905, 139 x 218 cm.

The painter, Hendrik Willem Mesdag, was 'a man of little imagination', according to one critic. Being a Dutchman, the latter most likely did not intend his comment to be understood in a pejorative sense but meant to stress that the painter's main concern was to render landscapes as he actually saw them. After settling in the Hague, Mesdag took himself off every day to Scheveningen to paint. At the time, the place was still a simple fishing-village and he would watch and note down the scenes of everyday life, the hustle and bustle on the beach, as the fishermen and women went about their chores. He liked to paint the robust wooden hulls of their boats drawn up on the sand. But, more than anything, it was the sea itself and its changing moods that seem to have totally captivated him. Although he was not a lyrical man and sought to reproduce exactly what he saw, Mesdag was – despite the criticism sometimes heard – too much of an artist to be satisfied with superficial photographic realism. Many of his works, especially those of the sea, bear the stamp of a strong personality and a highly sensitive observer.

Wendelien Schönfeld's painting in a way continues in his tradition, although she is definitely an artist of our times: the oil rig planted in the North Sea and outlined against the horizon is proof of a recent work, as is the loose brushwork and the strong hatching to accentuate the breaking of the waves.

Wendelien Schönfeld (1950), Sea, oil on canvas, 1984, 135 x 190 cm.

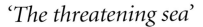

The sea, is it friend or foe? For the Dutch, it offers a love-hate relationship. In the course of its history, Holland can look back on an impressive record of flooding by the sea. Such floods have caused considerable damage to the country and cost many lives. Something of the turbulent power of the sea when it is unleashed is suggested by Marian Plug's painting 'Sea VI'.

There must, however, be a deeper layer of consciousness of the dangers of the sea which is completely special to the Dutch. Annette Kuyper became aware of it through a dream when she was painting 'Holland Memory'. 'When I was busy making this work,' she said, 'I dreamt one night that an enormous wave came rushing at me, engulfing the land and the houses and the people.' The drawing is built up of fragments of the world she lives in: part of a steel bridge, three windmills

Page 50, top: Annette Kuyper (1961), Holland Memory, mixed media, 1994, 92 x 122 cm.

Page 50, bottom: Marian Plug (1937), Sea VI, oil on canvas, 1985, 160 x 160 cm.

Top: Bart van der Leck (1876-1958), The Tempest, oil on canvas, 1916, 118 x 159 cm.

Bottom: Hans Bogaarts (1948), City by Night II, tempera and oil, 1990, 95 x 125 cm.

on a dike, a fence, a pollard willow, the front of a building. Along the whole length of the work, reeds wrestling with the wind catch the typical light of the lowlands – or is it perhaps that giant and voracious wave of her dream?

Bart van der Leck and Mondrian were for a time good friends. Both were innovators but Van der Leck never gave up visual representation. He used geometric colour planes to construct his paintings, giving additional strength to them by simplifying the forms. There can be no misunderstanding over the significance of 'The Tempest', which he made in 1916. It is a powerful work of art and yet as unsophisticated as a pictogram.

In the painting by Hans Bogaarts, the wave in Annette Kuyper's dream has become a reality. The man being washed away through the streets of a deserted city is no more than a disjointed doll.

Holland owes its very existence to the sea. Part of the country was born out of it, physically reclaimed and defended against its attempts to regain the lost territory. It has also provided the country with its main means of subsistence, turned the Dutch into adventurous seafaring traders and , at a point in time, made the nation at one time a significant world power. Fishing goes back to its very beginnings.

In the seventeenth century painting 'Breakfast' by Pieter Claesz., the neatly sliced fish is a herring. Every year to this day, in the month of May, the trawler that wins the race back to its home harbour with the first catch of 'Hollandse Nieuwe' is greeted with quasi-national honours. The herring is sold from fish stalls like the one in Co Westerik's 'The Fisherwife', in popular eating houses and in expensive restaurants. Raw, slimy and tender, with

finely cut onions spread out on it, the (decapitated!) herring is lifted by its tail between finger and thumb and lowered into a mouth, that is watering.

Boele Bregman's 'Women Eating Fish' captures them at the point of swallowing this delicious Dutch morsel while the cat stalks around smacking its chops.

Top: Pieter Claesz. (1596/97-1661), Breakfast, oil on panel, 1636, 36 x 49 cm.

Bottom: Co Westerik (1924), The Fishwife, oil and tempera on canvas, 1951, 87 x 109 cm.

Page 53: Boele Bregman (1918-1980), Women Eating Fish, oil on canvas, 1967, 122 x 173 cm.

Hendrik Willem van Loon, a writer of popular historical books, once wrote that fishing in Holland all began with a miraculous catch, like the one in the Bible. Even if his story is not altogether correct, it is a good one. According to him, this mysterious event took place in the Middle Ages, when millions of herring suddenly, for reasons unknown, left their habitat in the Baltic and swam southwards into the North Sea. Perhaps it was a change in temperature that brought them south. In any case, they must have found what they were looking for, because they have stayed ever since. For the Dutch it was a godsend. As early as the twelfth century, the fishing industry employed thousands of people and the discovery of a way to barrel fish and cure it with salt was to open up markets for Dutch herring all over Europe. The Catholic church forbade the eating of meat on two days a week and throughout the forty days of lent. There was no such restriction on fish and the Dutch were quick to seize upon this golden opportunity to develop a thriving trade.

Hendrik Willem Mesdag is unrivalled as a painter of seascapes. These earned him international repute. Here he shows the fishermen wading in waist high water carrying baskets filled with their catch.

In 1880 a fifteen-year-old boy made a small sketch which comes close to demonstrating the theory that the Dutch have an inborn talent for painting. The scene he portrayed shows fisherwomen, in traditional Scheveningen dress, loading their baskets onto a horse-drawn cart. From there the fish will be taken to the market. Inspite of his precocious talent as a draughtsman, Karel Johannes Cornelis del Court van Krimpen – for that was the lad's name – never took up painting as a profession. He did, however, pass on his gift to his great granddaughter Annabel König, whose work appears further on.

Along areas of the coast backed by dunes, all the fishing-related activities were carried out on the beach. The fishing vessels were even built there in special sheds. The boats had flat bottoms and when

they returned from the sea they were hauled up to the beach.

'Pulling down the Fishing-boat' by Paulus Constantijn La Fargue, who was active during the second half of the eighteenth century, gives a good idea of how fishermen were obliged to drag their vessel across the sand before they could set sail again. No fewer than four horses are pulling as hard as they can and being urged on with the whip, while the men are also putting their backs to the job. The next stage is to get the boat sea-borne. The nineteenth century artist Petrus Johannes Schotel chose to portray the very moment when the vessel lifts on the first waves. The sails are being hoisted and one of the crew is putting the rudder into place as another clambers on board. The artist is not devoid of humour. In the foreground, with his back turned to the scene of departure, a figure is playing with a toy fishing boat attached to a piece of string. A balding man runs to join him. He also has a little boat tucked under his arm!

Page 54, left: Hendrik Willem Mesdag (1831-1915), Unloading the Fish, detail, 1872

Page 54, right: Karel Johannes Cornelis del Court van Krimpen (1865-1954), untitled, pastel, 1880, 15 x 20 cm.

Top: Petrus Johannes Schotel (1808-1865), Bluff-bowed Fishing-boat before the Scheveningen Coast, detail, watercolour, mid 19th century

Bottom: Paulus Constantijn La Fargue (1729-1782), Pulling down a Fishing-boat, drawing, (second half 18th century), 21.6 x 38 cm.

Jan van Spronsen (1932), Offshore Fishing, oil on canvas, 1989, 120 x 80 cm.

Eventually, the dunes were pierced and canals were built to allow access to deep-water harbours behind them. This meant that the flat-bottomed boats had to be replaced by keeled luggers, a change, which among other things greatly reduced the risk of capsizing in a rough sea.

The forms in Jan van Spronsen's composition 'Offshore Fishing' are square and solid, heightening the impression of a trawler chopping its way through the waves. The clouds also stand out firmly against the sky. Seagulls shriek as they circle around the boat and there is a school of herring in the deep waters. They are green like the sea itself.

The Dutch also turned to whale hunting. They were very successful at it and in 1680, a whaling expedition with no less than 260 ships left for the arctic waters of the north. Sometimes a stray whale would get itself stranded on one of the Dutch beaches and this naturally drew a crowd of curious onlookers. There was even a popular belief that such an event was an omen. In 1598 a sperm whale of gigantic proportions – it measured fifteen metres – was washed ashore at Berkheyde, near the Hague, on the coast between Katwijk and Scheveningen. The appearance of this sea monster in the heat of the struggle against Spain triggered off popular superstition and was seen by many as a sign associated with the vicissitudes of the war. It was also referred to by history writers, who thus contributed to the creation of a powerful mythology of the whale. The fact that the event was repeated in the course of the next century only strengthened the belief in some supernatural portent. The Berkheyde whale was beautifully portrayed by Hendrick Goltzius and his drawing was afterwards turned into an engraving by his pupil, Jacob Matham. The artist, however, made at least one anatomical error, somehow confusing the nearly man-sized fin with a huge ear!

More than half a century later, Jan van Goyen, who always seems to have been in on the action, made a thumbnail sketch of one of these animals after it had been washed ashore. It is a brilliant show of draughtsmanship, in which the artist has succeeded perfectly in conveying the creature's sheer size and mass in the very reduced space of a small sketch-pad.

Jan van Goyen (1596-1656), Stranded Whale on the Beach, drawing black chalk, ca. 1650/1651, 12.5 x 23.7 cm.

Hendrick Goltzius (1558-1617), Whale stranded at Berkhey, 1598

Ellen van Toor (1958), Fish from Delft, collage-mixed, 1992, 60 x 80 cm.

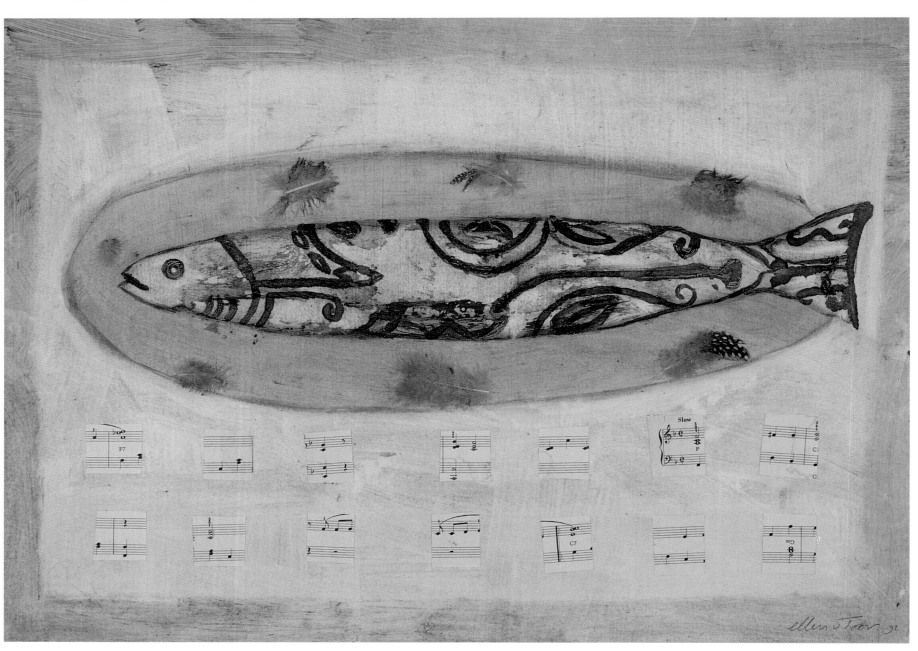

Much of Ellen van Toor's work is associated with the sea. She was born in Vlaardingen near the port of Rotterdam. The area has been inhabited before 2000 B.C., when the people who lived here scraped together a bare living from hunting and fishing.

'Fish from Delft' is a poetic mixed media/collage which relates to a whimsical tale about a fish that lived in the deep waters of the North Sea: 'One day, a Dutch fisherman caught it and took it back home. When he was about to eat the fish, it turned into china. And of course the china was blue Delft.' The story might have ended differently had Ilja Walraven's cat happened to wander into the dining-room!

Ilja Walraven (1959), Cat, acrylic, oil and charcoal on canvas, 1993, 135 x 170 cm.

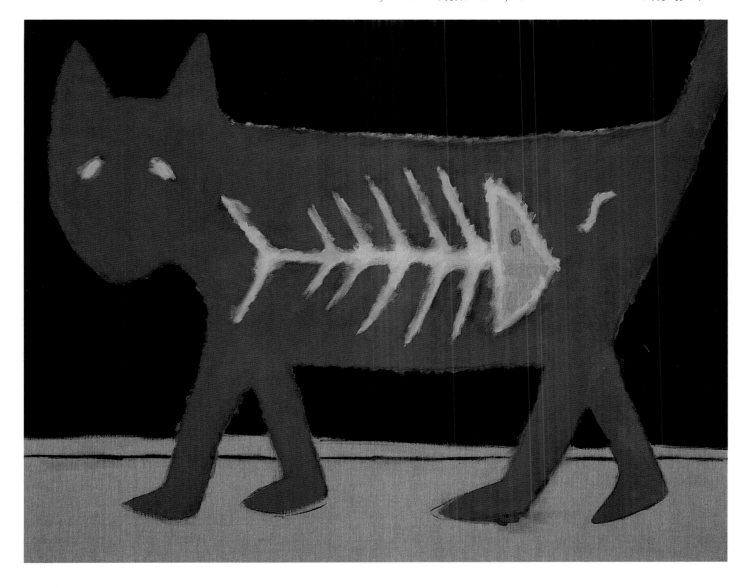

Trade developed on par with fishing. Here again, the sea played the key role. By the time the Republic of the Seven United Provinces had become fully recognised in 1648, trade by sea had raised the country's status to that of a world power. The Provinces themselves possessed practically no natural resources: the rivers provided clay to build brick houses, there was peat for fuel and, besides being fishermen, the Dutch were excellent farmers. Commercial appetite coupled with naval power was to supplement the little the Dutch had at home. Scarcity had trained them to make a profit on a narrow margin and tough bargaining became their hallmark. Much of the salt needed to preserve the herring for export came from France and Portugal. French and German wines were imported, and ex-

cellent beer could be obtained from Germany. The granaries were stacked with wheat from the Baltic, where the Dutch also found the wood required for ship building. Although there were hardly any sheep in the Low Countries, the textile industry was booming. It all really amounted to making a virtue of necessity. What the Dutch did not have at home they simply fetched from elsewhere, even if it meant sailing to the four corners of the earth. And once it was in their possession, the product was resold either in its natural state or after processing to give it added value.

It was towards the end of the sixteenth century that the great maritime adventure really took off. There was hardly a spot on the globe that the Dutch did not explore. At the beginning of the seventeenth century, a large number of ship owners joined forces and founded the mighty 'Vereenigde Oostindische Compagnie' (The United East India Company), or VOC, followed by the 'Westindische Compagnie'. Right from the start, the directors of the VOC claimed to have 40 ships manned by 5000 men in Asia, 20 ships with 400 men off the coast of Guinea, 100 ships with 1800 men in the West Indies, and an additional large number of ships and men in European waters. In 1619 the Dutch established themselves in Batavia (Jakarta, the present-day capital of Indonesia), where they laid the foundations of a thriving trade in spices and a vast colonial empire. They ousted their rivals in other centres and scoured the seven seas in search of new and lucrative markets. Their journeys took them as far afield as New Guinea, Australia and New Zealand. In the Atlantic, the Dutch settled in South Africa and in North America; in 1623 they built New Amsterdam, which was later to become New York. They also took possession of Brazil and the Caribbean islands. They dealt in furs, skins, sugar and coffee; they also played a less glorious part as feared slave-traders plying to and fro between Africa and South America, making huge profits and selling their 'black

Abraham Storck (1644-1708), VOC Frigate Peter and Paul on the IJ – Amsterdam, oil on canvas, ca. 1698, 85.8 x 111.3 cm.

ivory' to work on the plantations. The proud vessels that carried the Dutch to these distant horizons were elaborately decorated and a magnificent sight, as can be seen from Abraham Storck's painting of the 'VOC Frigate Peter and Paul on the IJ – Amsterdam'.

Portraits of seagoing vessels were popular in the seventeenth century. Some of the artists were highly specialised and possessed a great knowledge of ships and the sea. The intricate riggings, the motley poops full of wood carvings representing strange animals, figures of the saints or armorial bearings and many other details are faultlessly rendered. These paintings certainly reflect an aspect of life which is in sharp contrast with the traditional image of dull propriety often associated with the Dutch. To this day, the myth of a hard working, austere and righteous folk is as much part of their reputation abroad as a carefully nurtured national self image. It corresponds to the values and religious convictions on which Dutch society was built. However, the reality was always more complex. When it came to achievements, particularly in respect to worldly gains, self-praise was not foreign to the Dutch and they could at times be unabashedly ostentatious about themselves

When Abraham Storck's made his painting, they were at the peak of their commercial power. The oversized flags flapping in the wind on practically every available mast boast of unrivalled successes. The condescending attitude of the other European powers had turned sour. The English were calling the Dutch names and waging war on them at sea. The unrestrained display of riches even grated on the susceptibilities of the Sun King, Louis XIV of France, and in 1672 he invaded the impertinent little Republic that was on his very doorstep. After that, the country's significance as a world power declined but its accumulated wealth persisted. So much so that some historians do not hesitate to call the eighteenth century – rather than the seventeenth – the true 'Golden Age' of Holland.

Cornelis Claesz. van Wieringen (1580-1633), The Explosion of the Spanish Flagship during the Battle of Gibraltar, 25 april 1607, oil on canvas, 1622, 180 x 490 cm.

The navy also had an impressive fleet to protect the commercial interests of the Republic and it was regularly engaged in battles at sea with other seafaring nations, such as Spain, France and England. Artists were frequently invited to sail with the fleet to make first-hand drawings of these naval encounters, like war photographers nowadays. They also were very explicit in their renderings. A present-day comic strip artist could still learn something from studying 'The Explosion fo the Spanish Flagship during the Battle of Gibraltar', painted in 1607 by Claesz. van Wieringen. Nothing is left out and if he had only added a few captions saying 'bang' and 'crash', the painting could go straight into a modern cartoon strip book.

In the seventeenth century, Amsterdam was not only the main trading centre and financial heart of Europe, but also the largest port. The city is still very important in that respect, although Rotterdam has surpassed it in size. Much of the old glory is still visible. In fact, the centre of Amsterdam is probably one the best preserved historical sites anywhere in the world. Times have changed and George Hendrik Breitner would hardly recognise many of the familiar sites he loved to paint. But much of the atmosphere round the docks on the IJ is still the same. This view of ships in the ice – a chromatic feast – has not aged.

Top: George Hendrik Breitner (1857-1923), Ships Stuck in the Ice, oil, 1903, 114 x 60 cm

Bottom, left: Ingrid Dingjan (1941), View of a Harbour, water colour, 1995, 50 x 70 cm.

Bottom, right: Ingrid Dingjan (1941), Europoort Rotterdam, water colour, 1995, 50 x 70 cm.

Hens de Jong (1929), Harbour, oil on canvas, 1988, 3 x 180 x 140 cm.

'Seaports'

By 1936, the harbour of Rotterdam was already Europe's largest. The port is in direct contact with some of the world's major ocean highways and commands the mouth of the Rhine river which forms a natural link with the German hinterland and some of the continent's greatest industrial districts and markets.

The beautiful watercolours of a dock by Ingrid Dingjan has a dreamlike quality. To quote her: 'When I paint ships my brush tends to drift and in my mind I follow them on their route to new horizons.'

Hens de Jong has made an impressive triptych which in a way sums up the significance of Rotter-

dam. She has not detailed all its thousand-and-one aspects: she does suggest them, however tens of kilometers of quays and docks, refineries and chemical plants; hundreds of cranes hauling up and setting down loads while crewmen lean over railings and look on; and down by the docks the strong pervasive smell of tar and oil fills the nostrils...

The Sandy Coasts of Holland

Jan Toorop (1858-1929), Beach near Domburg, conté and watercolour, 1912, 14.9 x 20.2 cm

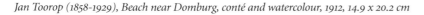

Dutch beaches as represented in paintings have two faces: before and after the development of seaside tourism. Towards the end of the sixteenth century, when the individual aspects of landscape were at last judged sufficiently interesting to paint for their own sake, beaches became a popular subject. Artists would go down to the beach, sketch-book in hand and note what they saw. Sometimes it would result in a painting. More often than not these drawings were spontaneous impressions most comparable with the notebooks and diaries of writers and they would possess all the freshness and intimacy of the first response. Many were discovered long after the artists' death, in dusty portfolios.

The drawing of a beach by Guilliam Dubois was probably made around 1647. The movement of the dunes set against the curling waves reveals a brilliant talent as a draughtsman and the animation on the beach has been exquisitely rendered.

Guilliam Dubois (1610-1680), View of a Beach, drawing black chalk, ca. 1647, 22.3 x 42.9 cm.

Anton Mauve (1838-1888), Morning Outing along the Beach, oil on canvas, 1876, 45 x 70 cm.

At low tide, when the receding sea leaves behind large patches of glistening sand, seagulls swirl down to help themselves to tasty morsels of shellfish.

The drawing, 'Beach near Domburg', by Jan Toorop, catches them at it.

At the end of the nineteenth Century, the Kurhaus Palace Hotel and health resort was built not far from the fishing village of Scheveningen. It became a favourite haunt of the well-to-do, where they came to fill their lungs with ozone and their stomachs with 'haute' cuisine. They were also advised to sit and soak in barrels full of salt water, which was supposed to be good for their health.

Anton Mauve, who was Vincent van Gogh's cousin and who taught him the rudiments of his art, painted this outing on horseback at the beach in Scheveningen. The lady sitting amazon style, the well groomed riders who flank her – one is top-hatted – clearly indicate that they belong to the upper-classes.

Soon afterwards other social classes discovered the pleasures of a day out at the seaside. Old people still remember the time when horses used to draw wheeled bathing huts down into the sea for swimmers who were too prudish to change on a crowded beach. Even then, they wore long bathing costumes that covered most of the body. After paddling around a bit and playing in the waves, the bathers would have themselves collected again, while beautiful girls lying indolently on the beach pretended, as they do now, not to notice the stares directed at them. The painter Ferdinand Erfmann was fascinated by these bathing belles, often resorting to a very peculiar vein of poetry to lovingly describe them. He once wrote : 'Snuffing and puffing like a rhinoceros, a heroic woman with mighty shoulders and sculptural forms, the bathing-cap and swim-suit glistening, rose up out of the waves as they tremulously withdrew having deposited their load on to the shore.'

Now, decades later, it looks on a warm summer day as though a huge bag of confetti has been emptied onto the beach: parasols, beach towels, children running around in brightly coloured swimsuits, hundreds of thousands of naked, shiny, sun-creamed, motionless bodies. Joanna Quispel has made a series of on-the-spot pastel drawings of the beach at Zandvoort. The scenes are real: the herring-booth drawn by a tractor, and the terraces with their display of sensually reclining sun-bathers.

Ferdinand Erfmann (1901-1968), Bathing Beauty, oil on canvas, 1961, 63 x 40 cm.

Joanna Quispel (1952), Zandvoort, pastel, 1989, 12 x 18 cm.

Joanna Quispel (1952), Zandvoort, pastel, 1990, 25.5 x 32.5 cm.

'A day at the seaside'

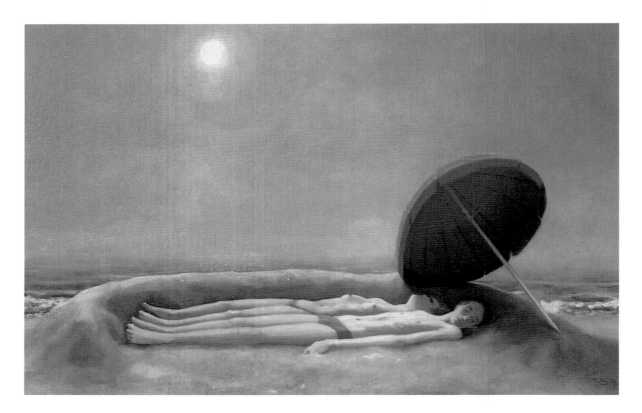

Hans Bogaarts (1948), Rising Mist, oil on canvas, ca. 1985, 50 x 33 cm.

Couples in search of privacy hollow out a pit in the sand and then entrench themselves. Even the rising mist in the background of Hans Bogaarts' painting 'Rising Mist' will not disturb their intimacy.

Michiel Kranendonk, a young, modern artist, does not seem to renounce the tradition of his illustrious predecessors. Both Ruisdael and Weissenbruch would have recognised 'The Beach at Schiermonnikoog'. It could easily have been the setting of Han Hoekstra's walk with his daughter.

It was afternoon and we walked on the beach
September and autumn on the lonely shore.
Driftwood.Bathers had left a ball behind.
Gusts of wind sweeping up the sand.
Far out at sea, a ship, moved past
Somewhere near the horizon.
Gazing as it passed from sight, she asked
'Where is it going to?'
Her eyes now questioned mine.
Seaweed, greenish black, a rusty iron bar.
SUNKIST, the print barely legible on the plank.
Nothing but silence all around
As the sea grew wilder, the sky turned grey.
A seagull flew ahead, and screeched and dwindled to a speck.
And again she asked: 'How quiet can quietness be?'

Han Hoekstra

Michiel Kranendonk (1966), The Beach at Schiermonnikoog, oil on panel, 1991, 29 x 63.5 cm.

'The spell of the dunes'

The dunes are more varied than might at first sight be imagined. Basically, they are just heaps of sand running from the most southerly point of Zeeland to the tip of North-Holland: a long, golden ribbon interrupted here and there by dikes and other engineering works. The Waddenzee islands, now separated from the mainland, are their natural extension. But dunes can be high or low, old or young, and with age, the calcareous content varies considerably and so does their growth.

Aldrik Sluis has fallen under the spell of the dunes around Scheveningen and Kijkduin. Narrow paths burrow their way through dense vegetation, like arteries in a living organism. 'The dune landscape is unique,' he says, 'a prehistoric setting just a stone's throw from the polders, in one of the most heavily populated and urbanised regions in the world'.

In North-Holland, the dunes cover a wide area and at times have an aristocratic remoteness about them. The distant view of these dunes by Gerard Wensma bathes in a late afternoon light which gives them a dreamlike perennial quality. These regions, around the year 1000, belonged to the Counts of Holland. Behind the rolling dunes carpeted with thick and dense brush lay a huge forest stocked with game extending from 's Gravesande, just south of the Hague where the Counts possessed their hunting lodge (which would become Het Binnenhof), to Alkmaar, north of Amsterdam.

Page 70, top: Aldrik Sluis (1948), The Dunes in Early Morning Light, oil on canvas, 1993, 120 x 140 cm.

Page 70, bottom left: Aldrik Sluis (1948), Dune Landscape, oil on canvas, 1994, 120 x 130 cm.

Page 70, bottom right: Aldrik Sluis (1948), Dune Ridge with Poplars, oil on canvas, 1994, 120 x 130 cm.

Gerard Wensma (1919), Late Afternoon in the Dunes, oil, 1995, 80 x 120 cm.

Ferdinand Bol (1616-1680), View of Haarlem from Bloemendaal, black chalk, Indian ink wash, undated, 14.9 x 21.9 cm.

'A mediterranean quality of light'

The drawing by Rembrandt's pupil, Ferdinand Bol, a well-known portrait-painter, shows relatively high dunes and the vivid white light that is often found in these sandy areas. It can have a glare that is otherwise peculiar to the south of Europe. Willy Rieser, who has often worked in the French Provence, also feels attracted to the dune area behind Katwijk and Van Gogh's famous painting 'The Harvest' shows surprising similarities with that same region. The hills in the background look like a row of dunes and the plain of La Crau closely resembles the fields leading up to the dunes. The group of painters who worked in the vicinity of Domburg in Zeeland at the beginning of the century had also noticed that the light in the dunes had some of the same qualities as that in the French Midi.

Page 72, bottom: Willy Rieser (1927), Dutch Landscape, oil on canvas, 1987, 60 x 115 cm.

Vincent van Gogh (1853-1890), The Harvest, oil on canvas, 1888, 72.5 x 92 cm.

Annabel König (1963), The Sun and Two Clouds above the Dunes, oil on canvas, 1993, 21 x 15 cm.

Jaap Min lived near the dunes. A painter in heart and soul, he has made an imposing series of landscapes portraying the dunes and the land behind them. The composition is firm and solid and the colours a delight to the eye. Two trees in the dunes stand out proudly, rooted in the sandy ground and holding their heads in the clouds.

In a recent semi-abstract work, Annabel König has painted the dunes on a summer day; she has reverted to extremely simplified forms and contrasting colours to create the brightness and the warmth they radiate.

Gerrit Benner was inspired by a walk in the dunes. His gouache has the candid quality of a child's painting. He is not depicting the dunes as they are but translating the feeling of the walkers when the sun is high in the sky, the light sharp and the loose sand crunches softly under their feet.

Hans Bogaarts has painted a man – or perhaps a woman – in a striped bathing suit, sitting in a quiet corner of the dunes and enjoying the company of a magazine and a transistor radio. Is it tuned to the news or to the 'Top Ten' hit songs of the day? A plane passing high up in the sky catches the sunlight.

Jan Moerbeeks very abstract work 'Meeting in the Dunes', is equally impressive, although it may not be immediately clear what encounter he is referring to.

Top: Gerrit Benner (1897-1981), Taking a Walk in the Dunes, gouache, 1950, 25 x 32 cm.

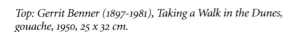

Bottom: Hans Bogaarts (1948), Hollow in the Dunes, Tempera and oil, 1987, 45 x 60 cm.

'*Strange encounters*'

Jan Moerbeek (1947), Meeting in the Dunes, oil on canvas, 1990, 68 x 73 cm.

Tulip Bliss

Jaap Min (1914-1987), Groote Keeten, acrylic, undated, 46 x 63 cm.

Dunes flatten out when they grow old and form a sandy layer on top of the clay ground. There couldn't be a better bed for flower growing. The bulbs root down into the sand without ever touching the wet clay in which they would rot, and yet the porous layer lets enough moisture through for them to become the most beautiful flowers. They have made the country around Haarlem, Hillegom, Sassenheim and Lisse famous. Tourists flock in their thousands to admire the springtime patchwork of multicoloured fields that stretch as far as the eye can see. An endless procession of cars with streams of garlands on their bonnets and bumpers drive through a landscape of neatly framed rectangles of colour. They are usually on their way to the Garden of Eden of horticulture, the Keukenhof, where their passengers will stare their eyes out in wonder at one of the most extraordinary arrays of different flower-species they will ever have seen.

The sheer joy of colour inspired naive artist B. L. Hoekstra, who earned his living as a grocer, to paint 'Tulip Bliss'. There are tulip fields further up north in the province of North-Holland. Their dense patch-work set against the rolling dunes was a subject that literally fired the imagination of the painter Jaap Min who lived and worked in that region.

B.L. Hoekstra (1890-1975), Tulip Bliss, oil, 1967

Queen Wilhelmina, the grandmother of Beatrix the present Queen of the Netherlands, was a proficient painter. She loved the Dutch countryside and at the beginning of the Thirties she worked hard at an exhibition to show her subjects in the East and West Indies what their homeland looked like. On occasion, she would plant her easel in the middle of the tulip fields. A gamekeeper remembered how he had been instructed to keep the grounds clear of inquisitive eyes. Even the bulb-growers were told to stay away during the royal visit. The Queen sat alone, a potent image of the sovereign's solitude, obliged to ward off her people in order to enjoy the company of the flowers.

Top: Judith Leyster (1609-1660), The 'Admirael van der Eijck', watercolour on parchment, 1643, 38 x 26.5 cm.

Bottom: Jacob Gerritsz. Cuyp (1594-1651/52), Blossoming Parrot Tulips, oil on panel, 1638, 38 x 76 cm.

The unchallenged queen of this kingdom of flowers, however, is the tulip. The bulbs were first imported from Turkey at the end of the sixteenth century and triggered a craze which has gone down in history as tulip mania. Reckless speculations in bulbs brought overnight riches to some and ruin to others. The flowers went for whatever price the biggest fool was prepared to pay: upto even, four and a half thousand guilders for a single bulb. The most expensive bulb was sold for 13,000 guilders: sixty times the earnings of the average labourer. Flowers became items of exchange. The English historian Schama recounts how the painter Jan van Goyen bought a tulip bulb from one of the burgomasters of the Hague for the sum of 1,900 guilders plus a painting by Jacob van Ruisdael and a historical painting by Judas van Hemsel. In 1637, however, the craze came to an abrupt end and the whole tulip trade collapsed like a pack of cards.

Dutch growers have bred an incredible variety of flowers: 800 different sorts of tulips, 500 kinds of daffodils and narcissus, 240 hyacinths and 300 types of crocus. These days, tulips are often named after famous stars of the entertainment world, whereas in the class-conscious bourgeois society of the Republic they were given the names of the military leaders, generals and admirals of the fleet of whom the Dutch were so proud.

Judith Leyster made a very sensitive drawing of the 'Admiraal van Eyck'. 'Parrot Tulips in Bloom' are by Jacob Gerritz. Cuyp. Jan Cremer is an altogether different proposition. His works rank high on the art market and he is known as a rough-and-tumble artist. His 'Tulips 1990-03' make a somewhat ironical reference to the red, white and blue flag of the Netherlands, while 'Tulips 1991' seems to be dripping with blood.

Top: Jan Cremer (1940), Tulips 1990-03, oil on canvas, 1990, 130 x 205 cm.

Bottom: Jan Cremer (1940), Tulips 1991, mixed media, 1991, 56 x 78 cm.

Land of Water

Hens de Jong (1929), Noordereiland, oil on canvas, 1980, 100 x 130 cm.

A quick look at the map of Europe shows why Holland has always been a meeting-place of races and cultures. Three of the largest European rivers have their estuaries on Dutch soil: the Rhine, the Meuse and the Scheldt. Since the dawn, people have descended these rivers and some decided to stay and settle. The rivers also form a natural trade route between the sea and continental Europe. The history of Dorestad, that was annihilated by the combined assaults of marauding Vikings and devastating floods just before the turn of the millennium is a typical example of the turn-table role many Dutch harbours would be called upon to play in the course of history. This prosperous trading centre was founded in the eighth century on the present spot of Wijk bij Duurstede (which still echoes its name) near Utrecht. To the north it was linked to the Flevomeer (before it became the Zuiderzee and later, in our days, the IJsselmeer with its immense polders). To the west the Lek river offered access to the North Sea. The Rhine and the Meuse ensured fluvial transportation deep into the heart of Europe. Fanning outward from this key position, the people from Dorestad traded with Denmark, England, Flanders, France and Elzas. Whale oil and tin could be shipped down from the Baltic regions and then routed on into the European hinterland, wines from the Rhine areas travelled in the opposite direction. The Frisian cow was already famous and there was a thriving trade in butter with the British isles. The extensive network of foreign contacts that Dorestad derived from its geographical position was a source of commercial profit but it also became a meeting point of very diverse cultures. Later on, in the Middle Ages, Kampen on the estuary of the IJssel and Amsterdam on the IJ, played similar parts, just as Rotterdam does today. The reason why Rotterdam has now become the largest port in the world is in fact partly due to inland navigation.

The Rhine barge on the painting of Hens de Jong is sitting deep in the water as she passes Rotterdam. As a consequence, dealing and meeting with people from many horizons, getting the feel of different human attitudes and learning to understand them has become second nature to the Dutch. To quote the former director of the Amsterdam Stedelijk Museum, Edy de Wilde: 'Holland is a crossroads of French, German and English cultures.'

The Rhine and the Meuse that used to flow north were deflected westwards by the glaciers which covered large parts of Europe in prehistoric times. The rivers now divide the territory of the Netherlands into two practically equal parts and the people living on either side are said to have a different mentality. 'Beneden de rivieren', south of the rivers, the population is easy-going, mostly catholic and loves the pre-lenten carnival. 'Boven de rivieren', in the north, they are thought to be more serious-minded and the majority is protestant.

The area enclosed by the Rhine and the Meuse forms a sort of mini-Mesopotamia, varying in breadth between 15 and 30 kilometer. Two important tributaries cut right through this area: the Waal, nicknamed the Inland Navigation Highway, and the Lek.

The young artist Michiel Kranendonk has made a woodcut of 'The Lek at Culemborg' where it makes a sweeping S-bend. The repetition of the cribs that regulate the current contrasts interestingly with the flowing line of the river.

Around 1650, Philips Koninck painted an impressive panoramic view of a 'Plain with Wide River' that could have served as a source of inspiration for Marsman's well-known poem about 'winding rivers making their way through endless plains'.

The Dutch were innovators in creating an impression of great space in their landscape paintings by using features such as meandering rivers. The illusion of space also helps to emphasize that man is reduced to nothingness in the vast wide world, a recurring theme in Dutch landscape painting.

Michiel Kranendonk (1966), The Lek at Culemborg, colour woodcut, 1993, 16.5 x 43 cm.

'*Winding rivers making their way through endless plains*'

Philips Koninck (1619-1688), Plain with Wide River, canvas, ca. 1650, 28.5 x 48.5 cm.

Daan Weyl (1936), IJssel, oil, 1965, 125 x 180 cm.

Jan Voerman (1857-1941), On the Banks of the IJssel, watercolour, 1891/1897, 35 x 47 cm.

The IJssel, a tributary of the Rhine, flows to the north through the provinces of Gelderland and Overijssel before emptying into the IJsselmeer. It has a long and eventful past. The historic towns along its banks once belonged to the mighty Hanseatic League and were important trading centres long before the development of Amsterdam in that respect. The air in this part of the country is clearer than in the marshy coastal polders and has a transparent quality.

With his 'IJssel', Daan Weyl seems to translate the eddying motion of a strong current and the purplish, rusty colours of the landscape traversed by the IJssel.

Spring has come to the IJssel at Veecaten.
Clouds and light, in changing states,
Give birth to a Voerman: an opalescent arch
That is heavenly to excess.

Ida Gerhardt

The poem by Ida Gerhardt refers to the painter, Jan Voerman, who spent most of his life working in the area around the IJssel. 'Every day, whatever the weather conditions, you could find me along the IJssel,' he recalled. 'Sometimes the weather was so bad that the captain of a passing barge would cry out, "And now you must go home, sir..!"' His 'On the Banks of the IJssel' is brilliant and is almost a literal transcription of the poem.

Hermanus Berserik (1921), Mist on the Scheldt, acrylic on plywood, 1987, 14 x 22 cm.

The estuary of the Scheldt can really no longer be called a river once it has crossed the Dutch border; it is more like a deep, wide arm of the sea. It is the entrance to the port of Antwerp and has in the past played a vital strategic role in the conflicts between the two Low Countries, Belgium and Holland.

An artist who has, more than once, portrayed the Scheldt, is Hermanus Berserik, an experienced sailor with an intimate knowledge of the sea. His 'Mist on the Scheldt' shows a tug boat in the foreground and further out to sea the outline of a liner or merchant ship in the fog.

So many rivers to cross makes bridges imperative. They come in all shapes and sizes: wooden bridges, stone bridges like the beautiful St Servatius bridge in Maastricht, iron and concrete bridges, swing bridges and drawbridges, road bridges and railway bridges. Their numbers run into thousands.

Pieter Pander's drawing of the bridge at Zaltbommel is impressive; a sweeping steel structure supported by huge concrete pillars.

An equally masterly drawing was made of the same spot by Constantijn Huygens de Jonge on 14 March 1669, long before the bridge was built.

It was on this very same riverside that Martinus Nijhoff wrote the poem 'Woman and mother' which many Dutch people know by heart. It is a melodic reminiscence in verse that bridges – as the drawings do – the present with a golden moment of the past.

I went to Bommel to see the bridge.
I saw the new bridge. Two banks
Which had avoided each other, it seemed,
Now become neighbours again. Ten minutes long
I lay in the grass, having drunk my tea,
My head full of the vast landscape –
When there amid that infinite space
I heard the sound of a voice, singing.

It was a woman. The ship she steered
Came slowly downstream and passed under the bridge.
She stood alone on deck, her hand on the tiller.

And I heard that it was psalms she sang.
Oh, were it my mother who stood there I thought.
'Praise be the Lord,' she sang, 'for His right hand shall save thee.'

Martinus Nijhoff

Constantijn Huygens de Jonge (1628-1697), View of the Waal near Zaltbommel, wash drawing and watercolour, 1669, 20.8 x 33.1 cm.

Pieter Pander (1962), Bridge near Zaltbommel, drawing, 1992.

'Landscape with a Stone Bridge' is a famous painting by Rembrandt. The subject is simple: a small arched bridge with a boat and a couple of figures. Rembrandt must have come across many picturesque sights like this one during his frequent wanderings in the countryside around Amsterdam. The French painter and critic Andre Lhote referred to this work as an exemplary piece of tonal painting: 'The subdued palette and the subtle changes from dark to light are typical of this approach and here they are done to perfection. Diffuse light is characteristic of Holland and the seventeenth century painters were experts in rendering it by tonal painting. The colours they often used were brown and ochre, olive green and white.

Top: Rembrandt van Rijn (1606-1669), Landscape with a Stone Bridge, oil on panel, ca. 1638, 29.5 x 42.5 cm.

Bottom: Willem Roelofs (1822-1897), Bridge across the IJssel near Doesburg, oil on canvas, 1889, 24.5 x 45.5 cm.

Rembrandt was such a great painter that he has been said to have been a 'master of colour' because of the beauty of his tones."

Willem Roelofs' 'Bridge across the IJssel' is a wooden one. The brush-strokes in this small painting are loose, varied and effective. The artist has used a circular stroke for the clouds and the trees on the far side of the river and irregular yellow ochre strokes for the little beach in the foreground.

The water is painted smoothly, contrasting with the vigorous brushwork applied to the wooden beams supporting the bridge and the railing. There is such an unpremeditated directness to this work that it seems most likely that it was painted on the spot.

Miep de Leeuwe has painted a cluster of moored boats on the River IJ with the elegant arch of a bridge in the background.

Miep de Leeuwe (1912), The IJ – Amsterdam, oil on canvas, ca. 1970, 95 x 125 cm.

In the absence of a bridge, the traveller may have to make the river crossing on a ferry. The number of ferries is decreasing as more and more bridges and underwater tunnels are built, but some are still in service and carry pedestrians, cyclists and motorists across the water for a small charge.

Salomon van Ruysdael (not to be confused with his nephew Jacob whose surname is spelled with an 'i' instead of a 'y') loved to paint ferries. He is known to have painted over a hundred pictures featuring them.

It is a well known fact that Dutch artists in the seventeenth century specialised in many different genres. The Dutch Republic in its 'Golden Age' had become one huge art super-market catering to the needs of the rich and poor alike. John Evelyn an Englishman who visited Holland in the 1640s, was astounded by the number paintings around and by their inexpensive price. 'Their houses are full of them, and they vend them at their fairs to very great gains,' he wrote. His impressions are confirmed by other foreigners who wrote accounts of their visits to Holland.

Salomon van Ruysdael was clearly good at landscapes. 'River Landscape with a Ferry' was an ordinary everyday scene and there is no attempt by the artist – overt or otherwise – to show anything but the familiar. Just plain reality: to stop and look at such a landscape and experience the exciting sense of recognition leads to a fuller understanding of the real thing. This is where Dutch painters were to be great innovators, setting an example that would quarantee a permanent stamp on landscape painting. It is even said that they invented it.

Salomon van Ruysdael (ca. 1600/1603-1670), River Landscape with a Ferry, canvas, 1656, 105.4 x 134.6 cm.

Page 93: Jacob Maris (1837-1899), Ferry, oil on canvas, 1870, 38.5 x 66.5 cm.

In this particular painting the water of the winding river is unruffled and mirrors a radiant blue sky. The clouds are at their Dutch best. There is a lot of activity going on as one might expect on a beautiful day. Take the group in the rowing boat in the foreground. They are having the time of their lives: a couple are hugging and kissing while one companion is pulling at the oars; another is slumped over either asleep or looking at his own reflection in the water. One man is standing, joyfully waving at the figure a tumbler in hand, on the back of the horse-drawn carriage waiting to be taken across the river. The other passengers in the carriage are more reserved; they are probably of a higher social standing to judge by the look of their clothes. Further downstream there are fishing boats. The ferry with its load of farmers and cattle is merely a fragment of the landscape, but so accurately centred that there can be no doubt that this is the real subject of the painting. It is also an excellent example of how well Dutch artists rendered and dealt with detail. The ferry is being both punted and pulled. The cows don't appear the least bit disturbed by the crossing. They are used to it. One of them is quietly drinking from of the river, another is rubbing her head against the railing of the barge. The scene exudes peace and tranquility. There might therefore be some truth in the belief that some secret alchemy in a name influences the nature of the person who bears it for the name Ruysdael is supposed to derive from the Dutch 'Rustdael', or valley of rest!

Two centuries later Jacob Maris painted the same subject. Nothing has really changed. It is the same boat and maybe one of the ferryman's great-great-grandchildren punting it across the same stretch of water. To judge from the cluster of trees on the right,the artist is looking at the scene from the opposite side. The pace of life continues to move slowly and rather drearily, as it always has done, imposed by the needs of a largely agricultural economy.

Karel Appel (1921), The Ferryman, oil on canvas, 1989, 120 x 180 cm.

However, the ferryman is also a mythological figure symbolizing transition.

In Karel Appel's scene of the ferryman, the world around him seems to explode. And so it did in Holland after World War II, in the Sixties. The country in which the German poet Heinrich Heine quipped that he would like to die, since it was the place where everything happened fifty years later than elsewhere, was suddenly caught up in a turmoil of radical change. The Dutch shifted the bulk of their efforts from agriculture and trade and became a top-level industrial nation. At the same time, many religious convictions and social values which had, for many centuries, kept an extremely tight hold on Dutch society, were suddenly rejected, joyously mocked and swept away. There was a certain amount of the neophyte's euphoria and condescension about these freshly acquired liberties, but the fact remains that a new society was born overnight.

In painting, tradition had been broken some years earlier just as abruptly by Karel Appel and others in a movement now known worldwide as COBRA, confirming the belief that art possesses premonitory virtues.

'Lakes'

In addition to the extensive network of rivers, there are many lakes in Holland. Some are natural but others are the result of extensive peat diggings from past centuries. Since the land is more often than not at sea-level or even below, it was never long before the peat-diggers' spades struck water. In the provinces closer to the sea, the country was badly scarred in this way and that is how many lakes originated.

On a sunny day hundreds of sails flit joyfully across the water. Sipke Jansma has made a dynamic and strongly structured composition based on this theme.

Sipke Jansma (1923), Sailing, oil and acrylic on canvas, 1988, 60 x 80 cm.

'Then with a blinding flash...'

Beside the smooth, still surface of the lake
blue and pink as moonstone
stand the stiff ranks of reeds
every stalk a living spear
and every spear in slender isolation
sheathed in varnished light.
Arrested light and shadow.
Violet clouds hang heavy
in the sky above.
Nothing betrays the yellow throng of birds
which populate the reeds below...

Then with a blinding flash
the heavens are rent and slam
with crashing violence closed...
As in a darkling forge there
bursts from the thicket of reeds
a spatter of sparkling birds,
an incandescent swarm of wings,
fly upwards in the somber vault of heaven
and loose the seething sounds of hell.
while the shrieking choir breaks loose.
My heart turned suddenly white and hot,
as if my very self lay on the forge.
In fear I endured the ordeal
and came away renewed and strong.

M. Vasalis

Willem Roelofs (1822-1897), Lake near Noorden,
oil on canvas/panel, undated, 25.5 x 44.5 cm.

Lakes also have an unfriendly side to them and an overcast sky can sometimes, especially if a storm is brewing, turn them into something quite eerie. In the past the angry waters would occasionally break through the dikes that were supposed to contain them and in the farmsteads around the old Haarlemermeer parents warned their children that the lake wolf was on the prowl again. Heads tucked deep down under their blankets, they would confuse the howling of the wind with that of the beast and dream of glistening white fangs and yellow eyes. There is something of that threatening atmosphere in Roelofs' 'Lake near Noorden'. The poem 'Thunderstorm in the Marshes' by M. Vasalis puts it aptly into words.

All hell has broken loose in Jan van Goyen's 'Sailing Boats in a Thunderstorm'. Van Goyen is known to have owned a small boat in which he sailed the Dutch waterways filling his sketchbooks with on-the-spot notations. He was not only a brilliant draughtsman but also a keen observer of nature. In this painting – one of several he is known to have made on the same theme – the artist has used an extremely limited palette. In a sense this economy of means enhances the lurid disrupting effect of a thunderstorm on the otherwise peaceful waters of a lake. Now, the little angry waves are jagged and white-crested, and for the hour come the wind will tear at the sails and whip at the faces of the men clinging to the tiller. A bolt of lightening flashes across the forbidding sky. It won't be long, though, before the water is calm again.

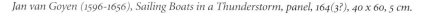

Jan van Goyen (1596-1656), Sailing Boats in a Thunderstorm, panel, 164(3?), 40 x 60, 5 cm.

In the Dutch nineteenth century outdoor painting, which in many ways continued the seventeenth century tradition, it was customary to fill in a picture with human figures or animals to make the scene seem more real. It would not have entered the minds of these righteous artists who lived in a Victorian age to include a nude figure in a wood and even less in a polder. Manet's 'Dejeuner sur l'herbe' would have caused an even greater stir in Holland than it did in France.

While seventeenth century Dutch society was moralistic, it was not prudish.

The bathers in Hendrick ten Oever's 'Landscape with Figures Bathing' are certainly farm lads taking a dip. It is a masterly if what unexpected Dutch waterside landscape.

'Getting Wet' is more recent but has the same sense of fun. Aat Verhoog, with his keen sense of humour, has portrayed himself throwing – or pretending to throw – a companion into the water.

Hendrick ten Oever (1639-1716), Canal Landscape with Figures Bathing, oil on canvas, 1673, 66.7 x 87 cm.

The Dutch waterside is the most beautiful place on earth because that is where I grew up and played games as a little boy.
My mother would tell me to be careful not to drown, and I didn't.
Nowadays my faithful dog barks from the same bank at the other side because she believes it's another world over there.
The Vliet – could anything be more Dutch? – is so beautiful because that is where I built a fleet with my friends to sail to the other side, another world we imagined.
But what do I care about the Mississippi?
The Vliet flows slowly in my mind and that is what makes it so dear to me.

Aat Verhoog

Aat Verhoog (1933), Getting Wet?, tempera and oil on canvas, 1972, 70 x 70 cm.

Skating on the rivers and lakes is just as much part of the classic image of Holland as are dikes, tulips and windmills. When winter comes, if the god of the skaters is well disposed, the shallower inland waters turn to ice. No Dutchman worth his salt can resist the temptation. The skates lovingly stored away when last winter's ice began to melt are now taken out of the cupboard. They come in different sorts. In one of his still-lives, Jan van Spronsen has featured two types, 'Friezen' and 'Noren', all ready to be strapped on.

Right: Jan van Spronsen (1932), 'Friezen' and 'Noren', oil on canvas, 1980, 90 x 80 cm.

Bottom: Bram Doorgeest (1889-1982), Staphorst on the Ice, oil on board, 1932, 50 x 60 cm.

There is so much to be heard and seen on the ice: the rhythmical scraping sound of steel blades on the hard surface, colourful groups happily inter-mingling, high-pitched children's voices, the clum-sy attempts of one skater contrasting with the effortless grace and speed of another.

Bram Doorgeest, a naive artist, has painted this little scene with a touching sense for detail. The three woman are resting and drinking aniseed milk. The skater sitting on the left has loosened her skates to free her feet for a bit. Standing beside the bench, waiting for new customers with a kettle in his hand, the man wrapped in a warm coat wears wooden clogs. They are probably filled with straw to protect his toes from freezing.

'Fun on the ice'

Top: Hendrick Averkamp (1585-1634), Fun on the Ice,
oil on panel, ca. 1615-1620, 15.5 x 29.5 cm.
Bottom: detail

Winter scenes have always been popular. Hendrick Averkamp, the deaf and dumb painter from Kampen, was famous for his pictures of skaters on canals and lakes, and had a sharp eye for detail. 'Fun on the Ice' provides a good picture of society in the seventeenth century. Just by their clothes and activities, you can tell the social classes to which the skaters belong. The two distinguished gentlemen playing 'kolf' would nowadays probably meet on a golf course. The game consists of hitting a ball with a stick with a curved end; the player who hits the ball against a post in the ice in as few strokes as possible is the winner. The artist has given careful study to the correct position of the player. In the background, two criminals swinging from a gallows strike a rather sinister note but in no way spoil the fun. Young and old glide past unconcernedly even if some of them take a fall. A horse-drawn sleigh stands in front of the farmhouse, about to leave. Special horseshoes with nails make it possible for horses to travel across the ice, but there could be unpleasant surprises.

*Top: Hendrick Averkamp (1585-1634), A Sleigh Accident on the
Ice, drawing, 9.2 x 18.8 cm.*

*Bottom: Andreas Schelfhout (1787-1870), A Frozen Canal
near the Meuse, oil on canvas, ca. 1867, 70 x 107 cm.*

Michiel Kranendonk (1966), Winsumerdiep in Winter, oil on panel, 1994, 29 x 50 cm.

In the drawing by Averkamp, horse and sleigh have fallen into a hole. The horse is attempting to get out, the desperate passengers are up to their waists in icy-cold water and a rescuer leans forward precariously to extend a helping hand, while his companion hangs on to him from behind to prevent him from falling in too.

The tradition of winter scenes has persisted. In the nineteenth century Andreas Schelfhout, a well-known romanticist, made quite a name for himself in the genre and his scenes showing skaters on frozen canals and rivers were popular at the time.

In 'A Frozen Canal near the Meuse', figures are carrying brushwood to be loaded onto a sledge. Once the job is done, they may warm themselves up at the 'koek-en-zopie' (colloquial for biscuit and soup) stall in the background. The scene has the typical pink glow of a wintry day.

Michiel Kranendonk works in the northern province of Groningen: a flat area with many canals on which skaters can travel endless distances. This is a deeply atmospheric winter landscape. The sky is grey and woolly. The two lonely skaters will soon be out of sight.

Ellen van Toor (1958), A Tour on Skates, etching/collage, 1990, 40 x 50 cm.

Providing the ice is thick enough, the whole of Holland gears itself up for the most important skating event of the year: the Elfstedentocht (the eleven towns race). Hundreds of people, old and young, put their names down to take part in this 210-kilometer cross-country race over the canals and ditches of Friesland. It is a rare occurrence these days – 'Winters are just not what they used to be,' say the old people, nodding their heads sagely – but when it does take place the winner is sure to be hailed a national hero.

Ellen van Toor has been listed as one of the promising younger artists in Holland. She is also a very proficient skater who has participated in the Elfstedentocht. The combination of artist and sportswoman has give birth to this subtle collage: 'A Tour on Skates'.

Hens de Jong has made a woodcut of a string of skaters that has a marked resemblance to the exciting pattern made by the dark figures of the Elfstedentocht competitors gliding through the white landscape of Friesland.

Hens de Jong (1929), Skaters, Woodcut, 1970, 30 x 54 cm.

Salomon van Ruysdael (ca.1600/1603-1670), River Landscape with Sailing Boats and a Horsedrawn Barge, panel, 1660, 45 x 68 cm.

In the past, the inland waters of Holland were an extremely effective deterrent to military invasion. The enemy knew that the Dutch equivalent of a scorched earth policy was to flood large areas of their country by piercing the dikes. Every Dutch schoolchild learns in history classes about the 'Waterlinie' (land flooded as a defence line), established to protect the country from foreign invaders.

Inland flooding has not always been deliberate, however. Rivers and lakes have regularly got out of control and caused havoc. The historian, J.H. Huizinga, wrote about this threat from '...our inland waters, mind you, no less than the sea!' As recently as February 1995, 200,000 people were evacuated from their homes when rivers overflowed and threatened to breach the dikes. Much has been said and written about these dangers but what would happen if the rivers suddenly dried up? The Dutch would probably all die of thirst. There is no water under the ground of the Netherlands and the yearly 750 mm of rainfall is hardly sufficient to supply 15 million souls with drinking water.

It can readily be assumed that all this water – the surrounding sea, the rivers that bisect the country, and the large number of lakes – have had some effect in shaping the minds of the Dutch, collectively and individually.

In many articles, books and in conversation, foreigners have often confessed to a degree of initial bewilderment on discovering that the Dutch are a far more complex people than they imagined. The widely propagated image of the Dutchman as a rather stolid figure, all 'of one piece' as the popular expression goes, has little relation with reality. In

'...our inland waters, mind you, not less than the sea'

his book on Holland, a Spanish ambassador referred to this disparity as 'The Dutch Enigma'. There appears to be a duality in Dutch people that outsiders cannot quite grasp: what the psychologist, Dr Chorus, has described as a dystone mentality, in contrast with that of people from southern regions who are syntone. In other words, there is a clear dividing line between collective sentiment and behaviour and individual feelings and attitudes.

Water may explain the phenomenon as the Dutch have been obliged to contend with it since their earliest history and this has fostered collective awareness. Proper, comprehensive water management has required a combined effort to maintain the extensive network of protective dikes. Floris V, Count of Holland, was the first to introduce a centralised organisation for this purpose. That was in 1288. What made it so remarkable, especially in those times, was that all parts of the population without exception were made responsible. The water boards who saw to it that the rules were kept were called 'Waterschappen' and still bear that name. They were responsible for a wide range of activities, including the coordination and control of damming and drainage, and the construction and maintenance of watercourses, bridges, dikes, etc. These bodies are seen as one of the oldest forms of structured democracy in modern Western history, leading, at an early stage, to an embryonic sense of civil duty. This has grown and is deeply rooted in the Dutch mentality. Collective attitudes are a noticeable factor in Dutch society and they never really lose them, even if they live abroad.

They do not, however, exclude their opposite: individuality. And here, once again, water has been seen as the formative factor. For water creates distance. There is room for individual freedom for people who are separated from their neighbours by water and it is interesting in this respect to note that the boundaries of regional dialects in Holland are often watercourses. These divisions caused by water in the past may partly account for notable differences in accent or humour, even today, between people living as close to each other as in Amsterdam, Leiden, the Hague or Rotterdam. Besides such physical boundaries, time also creates distance and remoteness.

For centuries the Dutch made much use of the slowest conceivable means of travel: the tow-boat. Originally, up to five harnessed men were used to pull the vessel with a towline. In the seventeenth century the draught-horse replaced them. But they did not die out completely until the beginning of our century. Some old people, even today, have childhood recollections of the tow-boat.

There were roads, of course, but they were built on marshy ground and carriages easily got bogged down. In this sense, water could also form the natural link between one place and another.

In 1527 when Lucas van Leyden (much admired by Albert Dürer and whose famous etching of 'The Milkmaid' is reproduced further on) left his home town of Leiden for Middelburg in Zeeland, he travelled by boat. It was simply the best way of getting to his destination. He spent much of his time drawing on board and sketching the landscapes, villages and towns he passed on the way.

By the beginning of the seventeenth century, regular tow-boat services had already been introduced but in the early days passengers had to suffer the discomforts of bad weather for, 'in this boat you seek protection in vain, against biting winds and streaming rain,' recalls one of the classic Dutch authors, old father Cats. Later, and well into the nineteenth century, covered tow-boats were a popular means of travel and could carry up to fifty passengers. All classes of society crowded into the cabin, which was filled with smoke from the long clay pipes: traders and peasants, prostitutes and men of God all got together. There were even special tow-boat songs to while away the time.

It has been said that the distance created by water contributed to the fostering of local autonomy, admittedly with a fair degree of parochialism. There is a collective community feeling. On the other hand, remoteness is also conducive to individualism; the Dutch have always felt free to live, think and feel as they saw fit, and they are proud of their independent nature.

The development of genre painting in the seventeenth century also suggests artists who painted according to their temperament and personal convictions rather than in accordance with a uniform model. Again, individualism might explain why so many Dutch painters have been precursors in their field: think of Jongkind's influence on impressionism, Van Gogh and expressionism, Mondrian in the field of abstract art, and Willem de Kooning as a protagonist of abstract expressionism. So water is after all perhaps 'the great divide' and the explanation of 'The Dutch Enigma'

Dikes and Polders : the Peaceful Conquest

Co Westerik (1924), Polder of the 'Unie of Waterschappen', oil and tempera on panel, 1970, 110 x 145 cm.

Round about 1620, an anonymous artist painted a wide panoramic view of Enkhuizen and the villages of Bovenkarspel and Grootebroek. The foreground shows the rectangular pattern of a polder landscape. The details, which include farmers and cows, have all been painstakingly added to the picture. The painting that Co Westerik was commissioned to make for the Association of Water Boards also shows a polder. It is surrounded by a ring dike and looks a bit like an empty swimming pool with three windmills on the left side.

Like his seventeenth century counterpart, Westerik could easily have based the work on the following instructions by the Czech writer Carel Capec: 'Take a portion of sea and build a dike around it. Empty the contents with a pump. Some of the best sediment of Europe has been deposited on the bottom by the rivers, as well as the finest sand from the sea. Let the land dry and sow grass on it. The cow will eat the grass. The Dutchman will milk the cow and make the cheese that is sold in Gouda and in Alkmaar. This represents, by the way, a perfect example of metabolism'.

In these few well-chosen words, Capec neatly sums up two important facts about Holland: firstly how polders are made and secondly, the typical Dutch aptitude for making one thing out of another, like the cow eating green grass and turning it into white milk!

Bottom: Anonymus, View of Enkhuizen, oil, ca. 1620, 60 x 138 cm.

'*Dwelling mounds*'

Jentje van der Sloot (1881-1962), View of a Village and Cows in Friesland, oil on canvas, between 1958 and 1962, 55 x 70 cm.

A few centuries before our era, the first to take up the struggle against the sea were the Frisians who had settled in the coastal areas. They built dwelling mounds on which to seek refuge during the frequent flooding of their new homeland.

Naive artist Jentsje van de Sloot has made a painting of a village on top of one of these mounds. It looks more like a rucksack on the polder but is nevertheless a convincing demonstration of the purpose of a dwelling mound or 'terp'. Peter Durieux's painting looks more like the real thing.

DIKES

When the Dutch want to express admiration for a woman, they often use the phrase, 'a dike of a woman' (they would never say a dike of a man). It means a buxom, warm-hearted, optimistic type of person. Dikes are protective and strong; they are something to look up to. If they had not been there, Holland – as it is today – would simply not have existed.

At first, long ago, dikes were just raised pathways leading from one 'terp' to another. But they also stopped further flooding and offered a degree of security to the land behind them. The idea of systematically enclosing large areas of land with dikes and then draining the water from the area within began to emerge shortly before the millennium. It spread quickly and a 'golden ring' soon surrounded Friesland, offering protection, as by 'day and night the salty sea swelled up against it.'

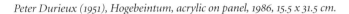

Peter Durieux (1951), Hogebeintum, acrylic on panel, 1986, 15.5 x 31.5 cm.

Master of the St Elizabeth Panels (ca. 1500), The St Elizabeth's Day Flood, oil on panel, ca. 1500, 127 x 110 cm.

When dikes gave way and collapsed under the pressure of the water, the damage was often devastating and it is hardly surprising that artists were inspired to record such events.

In the year 1500, the Master of the St Elizabeth's Panels made a diptych to commemorate the terrible floods that had occurred on 18 November 1420, submerging 72 villages. A year later, the storms struck again, this time inundating 43,000 hectares of land and causing havoc and destruction. In the swamped land, reeds grew so fast that it became known as the Biesbosch, the forest of reeds. It is still there and has now become a natural reserve and a haven for thousands of migrating birds.

In the painting, the artist has depicted various poignant scenes: water gushing through the breaches in the dike and people trying to save their belongings and their lives. For some of them it is already too late and their bodies are being carried away by the strong current along with the corpses of their dead cattle. Besides portraying the human drama, the artist is extremely precise in his account. He has taken care to map out the whole area and all the towns and villages are named in the picture.

In 1651 the breach in the Saint 'Antonis dike at Houtewael made such a deep impression that Vondel, the greatest Dutch playwright of his time, wrote a poem about it and (in a reference to Roman mythology) blamed Neptune for causing it. The painting by Willem Schellinks retains a more everyday perspective, although he has also dramatised the scene. In his picture, a man is frantically clambering up the dike in an effort to save his life and we can clearly see the depth of the Van Diemens polder, into which the water is streaming. Jan van Goyen, who always carried around a small sketch-book, was on the spot to provide a first-hand account.

There were believers who regarded these calamities as a sign of the wrath of God and some preachers – no doubt in good faith – were quick to play upon their fear. Willem Bilderdijk, who was both a lawyer and a poet, wrote the following poem and called it 'Flood'.

Whatever the mother says, the unheeding child will not listen and they drown. Using this metaphor, Bilderdijk warns the reader that he may likewise be destroyed if he continues to ignore the love of God.

Page 115: Willem Schellinks (1627-1678), The Breaking of the St Antonisdike near Houtewael in the Night of 5 and 6 March 1651, oil on canvas, 1651, 47 x 68 cm.

Jan van Goyen (1596-1656), A burst Dike near Houtewael, drawing black chalk, 1651, 15.5 x 18.5 cm.

'When shall thou awaken from thy slumber?
Arise, arise my child, the dike has given way,
Water has invaded our home and rises every moment more.'
'Oh mother, I would just as lief stay lying tucked up in my soft eiderdown,
And my dreams were so pleasing,
Please let me be...'

Willem Bilderdijk

Hendrick Cornelisz. Vroom (1566-1640), Battle between Dutch and Spanish Ships on the Haarlemmermeer, 26 May 1573, canvas, undated, 190 x 268 cm.

The draining of large areas to reclaim land and turn it into polders was a relatively late development in Dutch history. The reason was a steep demographic rise towards the end of the sixteenth century. Previously, there had been little need for new land to accommodate the sparse population. Around 1550, while the interest in hydraulic works was growing, Jan van Scorel, a talented artist in the tradition of the Renaissance, abandoned painting for a time to devote himself exclusively to engineering. He not only submitted a blueprint for a harbour at Harderwijk, and devised a machine to dredge the Vecht and the Rhine, but also worked out plans for water works near Zijpe in the present province of North-Holland. It is even said he spent a considerable amount of his own money on the project. Unfortunately, during the eight years that he held concession rights on the area, the plan

failed to materialise and his name has therefore not been associated with it.

The first large scale damming, draining and polder works were carried out in the seventeenth century in the Beemster, the Purmer and a number of other lakes in the same area. The man who was responsible for these projects was Leeghwater, an appropriate name as it literally means 'low water'. The windmill had by now made its appearance, providing the means to pump out large quantities of water with relative ease. Land speculation also played an important part: reclamation had become an interesting investment and in the course of the seventeenth century extensive lakes in the present province of North-Holland were drained and turned into fertile pasture lands. The windmill became a permanent feature of the Dutch landscape.

A later and much more ambitious plan was the large-scale draining of the Haarlemmermeer in the nineteenth century. People crossing todays densely populated province of South-Holland will find it hard to believe that fierce naval battles were once fought right where they are probably standing. Yet Hendrick Cornelisz. Vroom's painting is an eye-witness reconstruction that leaves no possible room for doubt. The lake had reached the dangerous size of 16,000 hectares. If the north wind blew hard enough, the waves carried as far as Leiden and a good southwester pushed them to the very outskirts of Amsterdam. By this time the steam engine had been invented and three giant pumping-stations could be set up to empty this vast body of water. A 60-km ring dike was constructed around the area to be drained and four years later, in 1852, the operation was completed.

The draining of the Haarlemmermeer was the dress rehearsal for a still larger enterprise: the closure of the Zuiderzee. But before the decision could be taken, a lot of thought and planning went into establishing just how it should be done. Numerous ideas were submitted, some of them quite fantastic, like linking all the Waddenzee islands together and draining the area within.

The Zuiderzee had come into existence some six centuries before, when a raging storm broke through the coastline into the huge enclosed Flevomeer just behind it. The gap had remained ever since and the Zuiderzee had become the entrance to the port of Amsterdam and to a large number of thriving ports all along its edges.

The plan that was finally adopted consisted of building a solid dam, 32 kilometer in length, the 'Afsluitdijk', that would literally cork the entrance of the Zuiderzee. It took twelve years to build and was completed in 1932. The construction of the dam started from both sides and was continued until the two ends met. As the distance between them narrowed, the current grew stronger and the final gap had to be filled at the precise moment when the tide turned. Once this last delicate operation had been achieved, the sea was finally excluded and a start could be made on the reclamation of large polders in the enclosed area.

A number of painters were duly impressed by the magnitude of the project.

Roland Koning remembered how he used to scramble up the construction sites to get nearer to the workmen: 'It was an extraordinary experience. They worked from both sides and the arms of the dam kept getting closer. The workmen couldn't understand what interested me so much. 'I know what I would do in your place if I could get out of here,' one of them once remarked good-naturedly.'

'Getting to grips'

Roeland Koning (1898-1985), Workers Building the Dike, oil on canvas, undated, 25.2 x 33.8 cm.

Dirk Nijland (1881-1955), Zuiderzee Works, two photo-lithographs of chalk drawings, 1930.

In one of the chalk drawing by Dirk Nijland, the workmen's boots are turned upside down and stuck on posts awaiting their owners.

At the North-Holland end of the Afsluitdijk, a statue has since been erected in honour of the engineer Cornelis Lely, the author of the Zuiderzee plan. He must often have stood there. What thoughts crossed his mind? Perhaps the same as that of one of the character's in the novel 'Het Noorderlicht' by F. Bordewijk: 'Yes, to be sure, the size, but the purity as well and the sheer simplicity. A dike illustrates how beautiful a single straight line can be in a world of constant change. The dikes are our lines of defence and we have built them all over our country.'

The line of a dike is also the subject of a painting by Jan Kuiper. But there is a worried wrinkle on its brow and gradually the frown seems to fill the whole picture. 'A Wrinkle in the Dike' makes one wonder whether the dikes themselves feel quite as confident as the people living behind them that they can contain the water surging against their sides.

Jan Kuiper (1928), A Wrinkle in the Dike, oil on panel, 1988, 95 x 78.5 cm.

The Delta Plan beats all the previous water control projects in terms of size, cost and complexity. A decision had long been pending to build dikes to link up the islands of South-Holland and Zeeland. Shortened by some 700 kilometer the irregular coastline would then form a solid and far less vulnerable front against the sea. The risk of flooding would be reduced to practically zero.

But in 1953, before anything had been done, a violent Spring-tide storm struck the southwestern regions of the country, causing the loss of 1800 lives and considerable damage. Flooding affected more than 70,000 people, drowned tens of thousands of cattle and covered vast areas of land. Eppo Doeve painted an impressive scene of the flood, a mixture of social realism and melodrama probably better suited to express human tragedy of such proportions than any factual rendering would have been.

Following a catastrophe of this magnitude, immediate action was now clearly called for and further delay as a result of a lack of plans was

Top: Eppo Doeve (1907-1981), The 1953 Flood, gouache, 1953.

Right: Ap Sok (1917), Delta Works, litho, 1962, 65.3 x 50.2 cm.

unnecessary. Some six hundred reports containing various solutions had been shelved because of the cost, so far judged prohibitive, and hundreds of tidal calculations and model tests had already been carried out. On 5 November 1957, the Dutch government passed a bill sanctioning the closure of the sea-arms in the South-West of the country with massive barrier dams and a number of secondary ones. In this way, it was felt, that at long last, the coast would become invulnerable to the onslaughts of the sea.

Henk Huig's etching shows the onset of the construction works. As yet nothing much is going on. There is a giant steel tubing waiting to be used, a truck and a dredging machine, a pile of sand. Not a human being is in sight. It is the kind of disorder and stillness that precedes an explosion of activity.

The sheer size and intricacy of the engineering works can only be suggested, and that is what Ap Sok has sought to do in his woodcuts: black-and-white patterns that reveal the complex fabric of the huge angular metal and structural beams.

'The Delta Plan'

Top: Henk Huig (1934), Vrouwenpolder IV, etching-aquatint, 1959, 35 x 44.5 cm.

Bottom: Ap Sok (1917), Delta Works, litho, 1962, 65.3 x 50.2 cm.

Charley Toorop (1891-1955), Dike and Sea at Westkapelle, oil on canvas, 1925, 68 x 78 cm.

The sea dikes are sturdy in order to resist constant battering by the waves and burrowing tides. Boxers are trained to step back to ride a punch and diminish the force of the blow. For much the same reason, sea dikes are built with a backward slant so that the waves have lost much of their force by the time they have reached the top.

In Charley Toorop's painting 'Dike and Sea at Westkapelle', the slant is visible. The workmen lean on their spades as they take a break and a ship rides the waves in the open sea.

Hermanus Berserik's 'Westerschelde' shows a mole being built out into the sea. The passing boat is a good indication of its size and the clearly visible layers within the structure make it look like a cross-section drawing.

Hermanus Berserik (1921), Westerschelde, acrylic on canvas, 1978, 30 x 40 cm.

River dikes can be quite lean and elegant. At their foot, and seemingly unaware that they are well below the level of the water flowing above their heads, people live unconcernedly in farms and houses. 'The Marriage Procession on a Westfrisian Dike' by naive artist Cornelis de Geus shows how far beneath the top of the dike life goes on.

Otto Dickes' drawing is a good exercise in correct proportions: the height of the river dike can be established by comparing it to the houses topping it and to the little figure on the riverside.

Jan van Spronsen loves the riverside and to cycle along a river dike. Sometimes he paints on the spot, while at other times he jots down impressions to

work out later in his studio. 'The Vliet' was made in this way. The subject is nothing spectacular, but has enough for a good painting: a narrow dike-road, a bicycle leaning up against a shed and behind it, the stern of a barge.

Hermanus Berserik is also a fervent outdoor painter. Even when his subjects are restricted to fragments of reality they conjure up the Dutch landscape he knows so well as a whole. Here, he has planted his easel overlooking the corner of a polder enclosed by ditches. The protective dike on the background rising to the level of the roofs behind it strongly conveys the sensation of being in sunken territory.

Page 124, top: Hermanus Berserik (1921), Old Harbour at Tholen, acrylic on plywood, 1994, 19.5 x 25.5 cm.

Page 124, bottom: Otto Dicke (1918-1984), Between Zwijndrecht and Heerjansdam, drawing, 1968.

Top: Jan van Spronsen (1932), Along The Vliet, oil on canvas, 1993, 100 x 85 cm.

Bottom: Cornelis de Geus, The Marriage Procession on the Westfrisian Dike, oil on canvas, 1979, 42 x 53 cm.

An aerial view of the polders looks like a surveyor's map: lakes and waterways, urban agglomerations, a wood here and there, meadows and arable land. The coastal regions in particular resemble a geometrical patchwork, carefully divided up into thousands of rectangles and triangles. As soon as the sun shines, some polders take on the colour of freshly mown lawns, while others are interspersed with the gold of the cornfields. All of them are hemmed in by silver ditches and canals.

It would be a serious misconception, however, to conclude that polders simply come off the production line. Polders belong to a large family and their ancestry reaches far back in time. The older polders are quite different in appearance from the more recent ones; polders reclaimed from the sea and those in lake areas do not look alike; there are polders consisting of vast fields, that unfold as far as the eye can see and others that are divided in mere strips of land by numberless ditches.

Jan Moerbeek painted such a patchwork. Even if it looks a bit unorganised, there is an strong geometrical foundation to it. It shows fields of all sizes, parallel running ditches and what might be ponds.

The watery aspect of a certain type of polder landscape inspired Jan Hendrik Weissenbruch to make this remarkable painting of a punting farmer. Wet land, interspaced by liquid surfaces, mirrors a very special brand of glossy light which has been brilliantly rendered here by the artist.

Jan Moerbeek (1947), Bird's Eye View, oild and sand on canvas, 1987, 125 x 90 cm.

Page 127: Jan Hendrik Weissenbruch (1824-1903), Polder Landscape and Punting Farmer, oil on panel, 1864/70, 24.5 x 36.5 cm.

Every polder has its own history and a host of peculiarities. Perhaps the most important common property is that they are all born out of water. And, wherever they are, water lies skin-deep and seeps up to the surface at the slightest opportunity. The polder is quick to moisten and turn soft, the texture becomes spongy and the grass that covers it glistens. In geological terms, it is a new-born child, a living organism. The boundless enthusiasm of generations of Dutch painters for this most characteristic landscape of the low countries indicates that it has always had a magic hold on them. From Rembrandt's day to our times, artists have painted them over and over again. Foreigners too have taken their sketch-books and easels out into the polders, charmed by the windmills, the canals and ditches, and the rickety old farmhouses half sunk in the damp soil. What they see is picturesque but whether they really get the feel of the landscape is another question.

Ger Meinemas' view of a farmstead at the far end of a polder is an attempt to portray the polder from within as a wide unbroken area of wet land running all the way up to the horizon.

'The Polder Pump near Zoetermeer' by Jan van Spronsen is also typical of such landscapes. A piece of heavy metal piping is half sunk in the wet grass and the muddy puddles are signs that there is too much water in the ground: the electric water-pump will soon have to be turned on. It does not take much for a polder to become a vast expanse of water again. In some parts of Holland, where they are as much as six metres below sea-level, some farms even have stalls in their lofts where the cattle are housed when the area is flooded.

'Born out of water'

The territory of the coastal provinces is barely more than a patchwork of waterlogged ground. Every Dutchman knows what it is like to trudge through a wet polder with the foot being sucked into the oozy slimy matter of the soil, the 'produce of the bowels of the earth' as someone once put it. No wonder that there must be a gut feeling among Dutch artists that gives them a deeper understanding of this land that they have conceived and nurtured. All around them there is a constant reminder of the harsh struggle they have had to undertake as well as the spectacular results these efforts have led to. It would be surprising under these circumstances if empathy had not had its say in the works of Dutch painters. And here, the object of empathy is the polder, the most characteristic and fundamental landscape of Holland, and it happens to be home-made.

The writer and painter, Toine Moerbeek, corroborates this view. His attachment to the polder is both visceral and intellectual.

It seems reasonable to assume that there are collective psychological implications for a people who has chosen to build a nation on such watery, amorphous and insecure foundations. 'Art is form struggling to wake from the nightmare of reality,' wrote Camille Paglia in one of her glittering essays. And, she adds: 'The modern artist who merely draws a line across a page is still trying to tame some uncontrollable aspect of reality.' Could that be the answer for their profusion in Holland? Deep down the people of this country are perhaps simply reacting to the very real vulnerability of the landscape they have built at great pains and against such terrific odds.

Page 128 left: Ger Meinema (1939), Friesland nr.2, acrylic, 1986, 140 x 110 cm.

Page 128 right: Jan van Spronsen (1932), Polderpump near Zoetermeer, watercolour, 1974, 42 x 29 cm.

Toine Moerbeek (1949), Buitenweg, pencil drawing, 1975

'*The polder sensation is extremely pervasive. I was born in a polder and for quite a period of time I spent practically every day studying it closely, making paintings, drawings and graphic work. In a way a polder is a framework, a flat surface neatly cut off by the horizon. As you stand within the frame everything is clearly visible. The distant horizon acts very much like the horizon-line in mathematical perspective. In fact, a polder could be considered as the natural version of the Renaissance peep-box. Standing there, I sometimes feel like the stage-manager of a magnificent spectacle as my eyes sweep across the polder. The choice of scenes and angles is infinite and, as I fit the elements I wish to view into the converging lines that run up to the vanishing point just above the horizon,*

I can decide on a close-up or on gradually receding planes. The illusion of being master of one's own perception is extremely gratifying. All I have to do if I wish to waive an image from my sight is turn my head, ever so slightly; and the trick is done. There is a tremendous sense of freedom to the sensation the polder gives me. My feeling of empathy with this piece of Dutch landscape is so strong that it has even become a mental fixture that I continue to experience indoors, at home. Here, my atavistic and carefully nurtured polder sensation has a broadening effect. I do not feel hemmed in by the walls of my room nor crowded by the furniture: the chair and the table become a willow and a poplar in a pasture.'

Toine Moerbeek

Maike van de Kooy (1951), Drowned land – Groningen, acrylic on canvas, 1994, 200 x 52 cm.

The young Frisian artist, Pieter Pander, has made a very interesting study of a bare polder. There is no green grass growing in it, just plain brown mud marked by furrows. Both Pander and Maike van de Kooy, another young artist who works in the neighbouring province of Groningen seem also to have actually used earth and clay to paint her polder landscape: a striking piece of work.

Although the lush grass of pastures, probably studded with dandelions, now covers Willem Roelofs' painting, 'The Month of May', his approach is also quite elemental, as though the artist was lying flat on his stomach when he painted it, enjoying the feeling of the cool dampness of the earth. The sparkling light makes the fresh grass look even greener.

'Earth and mud...'

Page 130: Pieter Pander (1962), Frisian Landscape,
oil on canvas, 1991, 100 x 120 cm.

Willem Roelofs (1822-1897), The Month of May
in Noorden, oil on panel, undated,
20.5 x 42 cm.

Piet Mondrian (1872-1944), Meadow with Five Cows, oil on canvas, 1900-1902, 27.5 x 36 cm.

On the same waterside, Piet Mondrian's cows might be lying, quietly chewing their cud. He painted them in his initial naturalistic period. It is tempting to see the germ of the highly disciplined abstract painter he was to become: the cows are reduced to little more than geometric shapes dispersed rhythmically across the dark green polder. Their backs and the ditch reflect the remnants of the dimmed light.

When the sky turns grey and the rains come, the air often carries the peculiar dank fragrance of rotting reeds and aquatic plants from the banks of canals and the muddy waters of shallow ditches, with perhaps a whiff of manure from the farmyard nearby.

Sjoerd de Vries' 'Tree in the Rain' marvellously encapsulates this particular atmosphere. It is interesting to set his work against the painting of a similar subject by the nineteenth century artist George Jan Hendrik Poggenbeek. It was made around 1888. Poggenbeek was a naturalist, known and admired by his peers for his innate sense of order. He may possibly also have possessed an urge to rearrange nature, a Dutch hallmark. Whatever the reason, atavistic of artistic, the composition is an exercise in equilibrium: the horizontal planes are balanced by the row of vertical tree-trunks in the background, and the diagonal line of the pollard willow on the foreground divides the painting in two unequal but faultlessly harmonising triangles.

'*...geometrical shapes dispersed rhythmically across the dark green polder.*'

Left: Sjoerd de Vries (1941), Tree in the Rain, mixed media on cardboard, 1974, 20 x 30 cm.

Right: George Jan Hendrik Poggenbeek (1853-1903), The Willow, ca. 1888, 26 x 22 cm.

The plane surface of a polder delineated by intersecting canals would be a rather dull place if it were not for its changing moods. There are no particularly outstanding shapes or forms, nor is the scenery awe-inspiring, although it can have a certain majesty. The appeal is largely immaterial and very much related to atmospheric conditions. Light, for one thing, possesses a spell-binding quality that is almost certainly due to the way it refracts in the Dutch countryside. The North Sea behind the high dunes and the broad inlets of the delta region disseminate a completely different light on the vast polders of Zeeland than when it is trapped in myriad canals and lakes as in North-Holland or Friesland. Light is pearly and glittering to the extent of hurting the eye in Zeeland whereas up north, where lakes are scattered like pieces of a broken mirror and there is no end to the canals and ditches, there is always a kind of halo above the polder. Imperceptibly, as the weather changes, so does the light; even under sheets of leaden rain the wet polder and the riddled waters in the canals continue to bounce back light spreading a pale glow over the countryside.

Kees van Roemburgh has caught the essence of this phenomenon in his watercolour.

There is another aspect to light that contributes to this feeling of immateriality in the polder. As Holland is a land of water, light is always vaporous and everything it touches is more or less veiled. This gives it a blending quality. Light tends to wrap itself around trees, houses, people and animals. The darker parts are made up of different hues of grey. There are no harsh contrasting shadows, as in southern climes, to carve out these elements in the landscape and create an impression of three-dimensionality. Colours magnified as they are by an infinity of particles of water, may have brilliance, but the same layers of humidity, however slight, also absorb and temper them.

Not plasticity but muted light and colour, and the changing moods they inspire, are a likely reason why Dutch artists have never ceased to paint so many variations on the polder theme. At heart the Dutch are poets rather than sculptors. Here the mind can wander and muse freely: sad or light-heartedly according to circumstances. On a bleak day, H. Marsman recalls his impression:

As the sky meets the earth
veils of mist, rich in hues
slowly smother the sun
and from every side
rings the voice of the water
telling the tale of endless
and dreaded calamities.

H. Marsman

'Spell-binding quality of light'

Page 134: Kees van Roemburg (1914), Polder near Utrecht, watercolour, 40 x 50 cm.

Jan Hendrik Weissenbruch (1824-1903), Canal near Rijswijk, watercolour, undated, 14.8 x 23.3 cm.

Since there are no obstacles in the flat countryside, distant views are made up of successive planes subtly blurring as they recede. In painters terms this is known as atmospheric perspective, and it is not surprising that Dutch artists are acknowledged experts in its use. Jan Hendrik Weissenbruch's beautiful watercolour of a polder landscape near Rijswijk is a masterly example. It is practically a monochrome painting, and this makes it easier to see how the tones become constantly lighter and more transparent as the subject matter gets further and further away. The cows in the foreground are compact and dark, the boat on the canal is lighter and the horizon is nearly transparent.

Life on the polder is full of surprises. Rabbits like to come and play around in them, there are rats and mice, and moles that burrow long tunnels in the fresh earth. The polder is also an ornithologist's dream. Hordes of migrating birds come here to rest. More than a hundred thousand wild geese arrive from arctic regions to spend the winter in the polders and swans grace the lakes and canals. A warming up of the ground water due to recent industrial development and possibly pollution may explain why the frog population has dropped spectacularly, but Holland is still sometimes referred to as a 'Kikkerland' (land of frogs). However, there are swarms of insects in the rich damp soil for all sorts of birds to feed on: the peetweet with its high-feathered head-dress, the red beaked and flashily breeched redshanks whose somewhat erratic behaviour has given the Dutch word for frantic ('ture-luurs'), the curlew that strides around on its long legs as though the place belonged to it, and many more. Ditches and canals are ideal for the grebe which uses water plants as building material for its nest. On the banks herons stand in absolute stillness waiting to strike the unsuspecting fish. You will often find one in the vicinity of a fisherman. It was not unusual for the masters of the Hague School to take their fishing tackle with them when they went out into the polder to paint, and Weissenbruch, among others, was a keen adept. Willem Maris made quite a name for himself as a painter of ducks. 'There is one subject for which Willem Maris was much praised and that is the ducks that he painted so marvellously well,' wrote a journalist in 1880. More recently, the poet J.J.A. Mooij, who was apparently equally impressed, also paid tribute to Willem Maris, in his poem 'Two Ducks in a Pond'.

Of course, they have come from far.
Driven by some obscure force to this peaceful spot,
They spread their wings and stretching wide
Down onto the smooth surface of the pond they glide.

Then time stops,
Stays endlessly still
Until by our gaze awakened
They once again depart on their airborne route.

Spellbound in shades of green and grey,
Cast by surrounding willows
And drawn by mirrored longings

Our senses slowely dissolve.
Then, as a spirit briefly floats in the air
Everything regains its place.

J.J.A. Mooij

Willem Maris (1844-1910), Ducks, canvas, ca. 1880, 93 x 113 cm.

'The pollard willow'

If trolls had chosen to live in the Dutch polder, they would probably have resembled the stocky pollard willows with their oversized heads and punkish hair shooting up in the air. When the thick mist rolls over the land, their dark silhouettes add a touch of mystery to their surroundings, as in the subtle and delicate drawing by Otto Dicke.

The pollard willow also appears in Rembrandt's etching of Hieronymus where he shows the saint sitting beside one: an amusing interpretation of a traditional representation that normally shows Hieronymus at a working desk with the dangerous carnivorous quadruped submissively at his side. The least that can be said is that changing the setting to a Dutch polder is unusual and that the lion must be feeling a little out of place!

Top: Otto Dicke (1918-1984), Ottoland, pen drawing, 1968.

Right: Rembrandt van Rijn (1606-1669), Hieronymus Sitting next to a Pollard Willow, etching and dry-point, 1648, 18 x 13.2 cm.

'*Painters at work...*'

Top, left: Hendrik van de Sande Bakhuyzen (1795-1860), The Painter at work in the Pasture with Cows, oil, 1850, 73 x 96.5 cm.

Top, right: Hermanus Berserik (1921), Lying Down, oil and tempera on canvas, ca. 1963, 75 x 65 cm.

Bottom, left: Willem Bastiaan Tholen (1860-1931), The Painter Gabriël at Work in a Boat, oil on canvas, 29.5 x 50 cm.

Bottom, right: Simon Maris (1873-1935), Mondrian Painting on his Bike, drawing

With awkward spontaneity which is part of the charm of naive art, Ilona Schmit has painted a scene of total domestication which overemphasizes the artificial character of the polder landscape: a pattern of rectangles in which the trees, the flowers and even the blades of grass have been planted at equally spaced intervals. The row of sheep, absurdly straddled by the members of her family, are also lined up in military fashion. Could the rider on the one single black sheep be a derogation, a hint by the artist that there might be some unexpected mischief in this landscape where everything else has been properly planned and ordered?

There really is a very busy life going on in the polder and it even provides a lot of simple entertainment if one is so inclined. Vaulting from one polder to another can be great fun...providing of course, that the pole does not get stuck in the mud halfway across!

'Surprises in the polder'

Left: Ilona Schmit (1943), Family portrait, 1977

Right: Sjoerd Bakker (1943), The Incident, etching, 1986, 48 x 24 cm.

The Windmill – 'Old Soldiers Never Die!'

*Charley Toorop (1891-1955), The Old Mill at Schoorl,
oil on canvas, 1919, 115 x 92.5 cm.*

In the perennial polder there is always a windmill, at least at the back of one's mind. Little imagination is required to understand that the windmill must have left a deep impression on the Dutch. For centuries they have been accustomed to seeing it in their wind-swept landscape, performing a variety of duties as far removed as grinding grain, sawing wood and pumping water; in fact, had it not been for the water-mill, their landscape would simply not have existed.

There is something almost human about the windmill, particularly when seen from a distance: the capped head, the solid, splayed trunk and the outstretched arms. When the wind rises and the whole massive wooden structure creaks and groans while the sails turn endlessly round, the effect can be quite hypnotic.

The German nineteenth century traveller Niclaus Lenau was far less enthusiastic in a letter to his fiancee Emilie Reinbeck. 'They send me running,' he wrote, 'I get sick if I look for long at their sails turning round. They make me think of a drunk stretching out his arms as he gasps for air and then letting them fall again. A horrible sight.'

'The Old Mill at Schoorl' could have served to illustrate his description. The wings of Charley Toorop's windmill really are churning the air. By contrast, 'Le moulins des brises' by Karel Appel is made up of rectangles and triangles.

There is a saying in Holland that people who draw too many windmills should be careful not to get 'windmills in their minds.' If that is a real danger, there must be plenty of lunatics among Dutch artists!

Karel Appel (1921), 'Le moulin des brises', oil on canvas, 1984, 196 x 190 cm.

One of the most famous windmills ever painted is 'The Mill near Wijk bij Duurstede' by Jacob van Ruisdael, but that mill is only one out of the hundreds, or even thousands, that appear in seventeenth century Dutch landscapes. And artists have never stopped painting them. Even though most windmills have by now become redundant, the attraction they exude still persists. Jacob Maris' 'Mill in the Snow' is a particularly strong watercolour study for a later oil painting. He has captured the mood of cold detachment of a winter day, and the dark sturdy mass of the windmill standing out in the landscape forms a sharp contrast with that of the bleakness of the sky and the snow.

Jacob van Ruisdael (1628/1629-1682), Mill near Wijk bij Duurstede, oil on canvas, ca. 1670, 83 x 101 cm.

'They turn on and on, taking with them my shredded thoughts.'

Leopold

Jacob Maris (1837-1899), Mill in the Snow, watercolour, undated, 48.1 x 34.6 cm.

If Mondrian had been a Frenchman, he might have analysed the forms of a mill and come to Cezanne's conclusion about nature: that everything can be reduced to a cone, a cylinder and a sphere. His interest would have lain in the three-dimensional possibilities of recreating observed reality using geometric shapes. But Mondrian was Dutch and more concerned with two-dimensional representation, believing that it would ultimately lead to inner harmony. To achieve this aim, he translated emotional values into vertical and horizontal lines, active-passive, male-female, objective-subjective, and into colours: yellow is active, blue is passive, red, especially if mixed with yellow to make vermilion, is health.

'Mill by Sunlight' and 'The Red Mill' belong to a series of experiments in this direction. The colour scheme of the former may superficially remind one of Van Gogh but the brushwork of carefully drawn verticals and horizontals hardly testifies to strong emotions. In the second painting, the brushstrokes are no longer perceptible. The mill has been firmly painted onto a blue background in which the sails cut out geometric planes. The colours have been selected to ensure just the right amount of blue to balance the vermilion-red.

Of late, Dutch windmills have been left somewhat to themselves: The Old Hunter, the Young Jan and the Bleak Death have practically retired since the steam engine and electricity replaced windpower. But in Dutch painting they will never lose their special place

Piet Mondrian, (1872-1944), The Red Mill, oil on canvas, 1911, 150 x 86 cm.

Piet Mondrian (1872-1944), Mill by Sunlight, oil on canvas, 1908, 114 x 87 cm.

Her Majesty the Cow

Pieter Pander (1962), Nude and Cow, oil on canvas, 1993, 61 x 68 cm.

Pieter Pander (1962), Denying Cow, oil on panel, 1993, 42 x 43 cm.

The priceless Dutch cow. The Dutch landscape would never be the same without her. She is a queen and that is how a French traveller to Holland saw her in 1927: 'Stately, motionless, the plump thighs glistening in the morning dew, blinking to keep the flies out of her eyes, she seems to be thinking as she chews her cud, "Holland belongs to me and those kind, friendly Dutch people reclaimed the land from the sea specially so that there would be grass for me to eat."'

The heavy udder shows how the cow has gained her reputation. Twice a day, the floodgates of the Dutch dairy industry open as a milking machine is attached to some two million udders. Annual production per cow averages 6,000 litres, a figure which makes the mind boggle.

Apart from being such a good producer, the cow is a favourite artist's model. Painting unclothed figures has never been much of a tradition in Dutch painting. Excellent nudes have been painted, of course, but the Dutch Calvinist background meant that there was never really a market for them. The cow has largely compensated for this.

Peter Pander has brought the two models together in one painting: a brilliant piece of work with a tongue-in-cheek humour to it. 'Denying Cow' by the same artist looks as though its subject has just seen the first two go by and can't believe her eyes.

When Lucas van Leyden made his copper etching 'The Milkmaid' in 1570, it was practically a premiere. In those days it was not customary to paint animals for their own sake.

The next step in the nascent young love scene between the milkmaid and the farmhand has been touchingly rendered by Cornelis de Geus!

Top: Lucas van Leyden (1489-1533), The Milkmaid, copper etching, 1570

Bottom: Cornelis de Geus (1914), Lovestruck Milkers, oil, 1975, 45 x 61 cm.

After Lucas van Leyden, Dutch painters have never stopped painting cows. All breeds of cattle have been portrayed, both the black-and-white Frisian, a milk producer, and the red-and-white beef cow.

When Conny Sprinkhuizen painted the latter and then heard what the real cow's fate was to be, she swiftly picked up her brush and changed the colour to black.

In the seventeenth century, Paulus Potter was the artist who really launched the fashion for painting cattle and generations of painters, through until the nineteenth century, regarded him as their master.

Top: Bert Osinga (1953), Cows near Hilversum, pencil drawing white chalk, 1980, 24 x 33.5 cm.

Bottom: Paulus Potter (1625-1654), Pissing Cow and Two Sheep, drawing black chalk, undated, 10 x 13.9 cm.

His world-famous 'Young Bull' is an early work. He was only twenty-one when he executed it. Potter spent many hours outside, drawing and studying the animals for his paintings. He observed them with an extremely keen eye and their anatomy held no secrets for him. As he was a realist and a Dutchman, he studied cows from every angle and observed every conceivable bovine activity. His drawing of a urinating cow, although almost clinical in approach, is remarkably well done.

Luminosity plays an essential role in the modern pencil drawing by Bert Osinga, with its strongly abstracted forms.

Conny Sprinkhuizen (1960), Cows, acrylic on canvas, 1991, 100 x 140 cm.

Never, perhaps, has so much attention been paid to the cow as in the nineteenth century, when outdoor painting became so popular. The painters of the Hague School seemed never to tire of representing cattle in their landscapes. It is said that Willem Maris used to go out sketching as a boy and that he once grew so absorbed that dusk fell and the cows assembled for milking without his noticing. He got such a fright when he suddenly became aware of them all around him that he did not dare move and go home. The experience did not discourage him, however, or prevent him from producing beautiful paintings like the 'Cow Reflecting the Light'. The cow is quietly chewing its cud and there is a nearly transparent shine on its white hide. Light is also of prime importance in 'Two Young Calves', where it is accentuated by the contrast between the white and the black calf.

Top: Willem Maris (1844-1910), Two Young Calves, oil on canvas, 30 x 50 cm.

Bottom: Willem Maris (1844-1910), Cow Reflecting the Light, oil on canvas, undated, 65 x 81 cm.

Perhaps the most touching animal painting in Dutch art, with the exception of Van Gogh's 'Old Horse', is the 'Lying Cow' by the eccentric expressionist painter Hendrik Chabot. The animal is lying in a polder with closed eyes and a trusting expression, as if she is waiting for someone to come and scratch her between the horns.

Hendrik Chabot (1894-1949), Lying Cow, oil on canvas, 1936, 94.5 x 153 cm.

Ilja Walraven (1959), Clara II, oil on canvas, 1992, 45 x 55 cm.

Anonymus, Bull with Zutphen on the Background, oil on canvas, early 19th Century, 44 x 56 cm.

Ilja Walraven (1959), Clara I, acrylic, oil, zinc and charcoal on canvas, 1992, 55 x 60 cm.

Paulus Potter (1625-1654), Young Bull, oil on canvas, 1647, 236 x 345 cm.

The cow continues to inspire young painters like Ilja Walraven. His 'Clara II has big, sentimental eyes. At the artist's request, 'Clara I' is also selected for inclusion here since she is, in his view, the perfect match for Potter's 'Young Bull'. 'They are twin souls,' he says, 'and if you look carefully they both seem to be floating slightly in the air.' The truth of the matter is that specialists have established that Potter's bull' was made up of elements of more than one animal: its rump is older than its front, and this would explain why it is slightly off balance. 'Clara II' has also been given a boyfriend. He comes from Zutphen and has the same melancholic, infatuated look as his new partner.

Rembrandt, the greatest Dutch painter of all time, appears not to have shared the general interest in cows. He did, however, produce a famous painting of an ox carcas in a slaughterhouse and a little etching of a young bull-calf beside a canal. The latter is so freely drawn that it is quite timeless.

Annabel König, who is a young and upcoming artist, has made a remarkable gouache of the same subject, and this continuing interest seems to indicate that cows are not yet out of the picture in Dutch painting.

Top: Rembrandt van Rijn (1606-1669), Young Bull, etching, ca. 1650, 10.5 x 7.5 cm.

Bottom: Annabel König (1963), Cows, mixed media/gouache, 1992, 20 x 27 cm.

To portray cattle, and cattle only, untiringly for decades on end is no mean achievement and goes to prove that the cow can form an inexhaustible source of artistic inspiration. Ever since she graduated from art school Marleen Felius has exclusively painted and drawn cows and bulls and in the process, has acquired an encyclopaedic knowledge about them. 'When I am at work painting a cow,' she says, 'I somehow inexplicably identify myself with my subject and become part of her. It is a fascinating animal of great beauty and strength.' It is feeding time on the painting reproduced here and the cows are gathered at the fence waiting for it to be opened. Only their backs and the black and white patterns are visible and yet there is a very realistic feel of large warm bodies pushing up against each other.

Marleen Felius (1948), Cows at the Trough, acrylic on paper, 1985, 55 x 75 cm.

Marleen Felius (1948), Evening in Friesland, acrylic/oil on canvas, 1993, 70 x 100 cm.

A Way of Looking at the Dutch

It is possible to single out particular characteristics that recur in the works of Dutch painters down the centuries and to relate these to a cultural identity. Assessments by art historians and, for that matter, by the general public, vary and are anything but final. Our view of the past is necessarily coloured, if not clouded, by the present. The way Rembrandt was regarded during his lifetime or in the nineteenth century is different from the way we see him today, when some people even believe that there are affinities between him and the rough-brushed COBRA (an international movement, standing for COpenhagen BRussels Amsterdam) painter Karel Appel. The artist himself seemed to be aware of some sort of kinship when he stated: 'I work quickly, nothing extraordinary about that. Artists elsewhere have done the same before; Rembrandt could not bear to waste time either.' They both appear to possess the same 'emotional drive', to quote Edy de Wilde, the former director of the Stedelijk Museum in Amsterdam. When asked in an interview, 'what do you think is the typical feature of Dutch art?' he replied: 'Holland has always – especially in its art featured two extremes: on the one hand there is an expressionistic emotional drive, Van Gogh for example (or Karel Appel today? – LFF) and on the other a tendency towards just the opposite: a highly disciplined form of art.' So, on one side of the balance there would be exteriorised emotions of the kind that ultimately destroyed Vincent van Gogh – in his last letter to his brother, Theo, he wrote: 'Well, in my work I am risking my life...' – whereas on the other, a Piet Mondrian's emotional relationship to art is one of control through objectivism.

Karel Appel (1921), Portrait of Willem Sandberg, oil on canvas, 1956, 190 x 130 cm.

If one were to look for more comparisons between the present and the past, a commonality has been noted between the abstract works of Piet Mondrian and the architectural paintings produced by Pieter Jansz. Saenredam three centuries earlier. The composition of the 'Church at Assendelft' where Saenredam was born in 1597, is rigorously geometric and so is the remarkable painting of roofs by the contemporary artist Gerard Wensma. Both have reduced the severity of form by the use of light warm colours: golden brown and a subtle blue coming through the church windows in Saenredam's painting and which is also the colour of the roofs by Wensma.

Top: Pieter Jansz. Saenredam (1597-1665), Church at Assendelft, panel, 1649, 50 x 76 cm.

Bottom: Gerard Wensma (1919), Reflection, oil, 1975, 125 x 125 cm.

Johannes Vermeer (1632-1675), The Music Lesson, oil on canvas, ca. 1662, 73.3 x 64.5 cm.

Piet Mondrian (1872-1944), Composition in Red, Yellow and Blue, oil on canvas, 1921, 80 x 50 cm.

The English author, William Gaunt, was also struck by an affinity with Mondrian in the use Vermeer makes of the rectangle of a picture frame, the tracery of a window and the black and white squares which pattern a floor, these giving a delightful sense of pictorial order to his 'Gentleman and Lady at a Spinet.' It is often suggested that these two artists' strictly structured compositions are the outcome of a calvinistic background and upbringing. To return to Edy de Wilde's definition, the same 'disciplined' approach as in the foregoing examples can also be observed in the unusual graphic work of M.C. Escher. His Dutch landscape 'Day and Night' is an aer-ial view that combines two elements: reality and abstraction. Escher has cleverly made them merge and even managed a third transformation back to reality: polders become squares and then turn into birds. Certainly a carefully devised composition and a highly controlled form of art.

The atavistic need for structure and restraint of the Dutch is also evidenced in a sensitive etching of a small ship at sea made by Jurjen Ravenhorst in 1993. The water is hemmed in by a square frame and this is not altogether accidental. The artist himself claims: 'If I had lived in the southern part of Europe I would probably not have done it. The need to order things must come from my Dutch genes.'

These two poles – 'emotional drive' and 'highly disciplined art' – never really get out of hand. The attitude to life of the Dutch is not revolutionary: considering the nature of the country they live in, they could hardly afford the luxury of excess – in any direction. Balance, restraint and measure are a question of survival. But as an undercurrent both tendencies do exist and, according to Edy de Wilde, 'the contrast is clearly discernible in Dutch art and is typical of the country's contribution to the arts in general.'

Dutch art is founded and built on realism. Even the most well known abstract painter of Holland, Piet Mondrian strove to achieve an essential reality. He began his quest by synthesizing and compressing nature as is clearly evidenced by his famous tree series. His opposite in artistic expression, Karel Appel, who is also a realist aimed at recapturing the spontaneous sense of reality of a child.

Mondrian and Appel are extremes. Mainstream art in Holland is a sober form of realism without superfluous embellishments. The English art historian, Kenneth Clarke, referred to a 'landscape of fact' in the work of the seventeenth century Dutch painters. Although they often reconstruct or rearrange their landscapes for compositional purposes when producing their final studio paintings, the elements were taken from reality and their sketch-books abound in on-the-spot studies. That is why looking at their works can prove to be such an interesting means of get-

ting to know the country and the people. To quote Ton Lemaire once again: 'What we continue to admire and value today in Dutch painting, in particular in the art of landscape painting, is that it provides recognition of the early forms

from which our present realism stems. Our particular realism has its origins in Holland and Flanders and what we admire in it is that it takes us back to the beginnings of our own visual codes.'

'The need to order things...'

Top: M. C. Escher (1898-1972), Day and Night, woodcut, two colours, 1938, 39.3 x 67.8 cm.

Bottom: Jurjen Ravenhorst (1958), Ship at Sea, litho black-white, 1993, 28 x 13.5 cm.

Realistic art in the Netherlands stems from the Middle Ages. It began with the richly coloured and finely detailed illuminations and miniatures of holy books and Books of Hours, recounting the history of mighty kings and princes. Jan van Eyck, who served in the retinue of the Counts of Holland in the Hague around 1422, is one of the greatest painters of all time. He began his career as a miniaturist and is the presumed illustrator of the 'Book of Hours of Turin', which was destroyed in a fire in 1904. Fortunately we still have reproductions even if they are only in black and white. On one of the pages, Jan van Eyck has depicted Count Willem VI of Holland landing on the shores of Walcheren in the Dutch province of Zeeland. The scene already displays some of the attributes and qualities for which Dutch painting was to become famous.

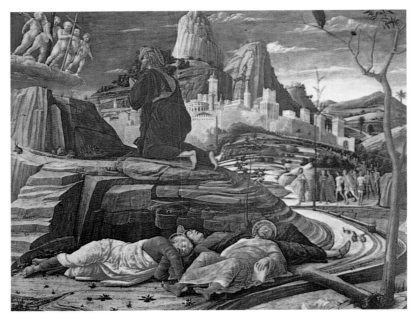

Andrea Mantegna (1431-1506), Agony in the Garden, painting, 1459, 63 x 80 cm.

Page 163: Geertgen-tot-Sint-Jan (1460/65-1490/95), St John the Baptist in the Wilderness, oil on panel (oak), 1485/90, 42 x 28 cm.

Jan van Eyck (ca. 1390-1441), Count Willem VI of Holland Landing on the Beach of Walcheren, ca. 1422.

First and foremost, it shows keen observation and love of nature in all its details: the beach with the boats drawn up on the sand, the curling waves, the swell of the dunes and the clouded sky resting on a distant horizon can be seen as the prototype of Dutch seascapes for generations to come. Secondly, it is small in scale. The artist required only a few centimeters to give a detailed and truthful account of the scene. It is very far removed from the monumental frescos that Italian artists were producing at around the same time. For them, composition, form and colour were much more important than details or psychological expression which could not be seen from a distance. Many Dutch paintings invite examination through a magnifying glass, whereas one has to stand back to admire the beauty of an Italian mural. This is a definite difference in approach to art, and one which in some ways reflects two different cultures.

Michelangelo, who was accustomed to paintings on a grand scale, was critical of the painters from the north who, he felt, displayed a tendency, to perceive the world around them as a sum of loose parts. 'This art of painting', he is claimed to have said, 'is without power or glory: it attempts to represent too many things at a time completely, whereas a single one would be enough to require all their attention.' No one today would dream of describing the Flemish masterpieces in these terms, but Michelangelo does make an interesting point by referring to the existence of distinct differences of attitude between painters from the north and the south of Europe – a case of explicitness by means of detail versus implicitness through general effect?

Economic development took place later in the Northern Netherlands than in Flanders, and the same was true of the development of painting. But it did not take the northern artists long to catch up. Around 1460, the Haarlem artist, Geertgen-tot-Sint-Jan, produced a painting of John the Baptist. It is a brilliant piece of work. Every aspect of the landscape – light, sky, trees and flowers – is executed with the utmost precision and in the finest detail, all blending in perfect harmony to create a striking composition. St John is resting on a rock. Perhaps he is praying, perhaps his thoughts are just wandering. There is something very gentle and modest about him. Certainly nothing to indicate the distance between a saint and a mere mortal. The way the holy man crosses his feet is masterly, and adds a touch of candid humour to the scene. The Dutch are allergic to affectation and the artist has successfully contrived to present St John as a simple, ordinary human being, just like the rest of us. In contrast, there is a remarkable picture by the Italian artist Andrea Mantegna who was active at the same time. It shows a scene in 'Agony in The Garden'. Here the artist sought stage-effect rather than naturalistic and detailed representation; the scenery is made up of blocked forms and the angels descending from heaven seem to be coming down with a rope and pullies. When the performance is over the actors playing the apostles who are fast asleep will get up and have a drink together at the nearest tavern. The Dutch love of detail has also been explained by reference to the climate. Humidity often veils the landscape in mist, forcing the eye to scan its surroundings more attentively and, the theory would have it, over time the Dutch have thus evolved a high degree of visual acuity.

A more convincing argument has been advanced by a well-known Dutch professor of psychology. According to Dr. Chorus, the wet climate obliges his fellow compatriots to spend much of their time indoors. So, unlike people who live in warmer climes and are used to being part of a crowd, they do not express their feelings easily, particularly in public. The Dutch, consequently, are an introverted people who watch through their windows as the flow of life goes by, sharply picking out peculiarities, and this has turned them into sensitive – if somewhat critical – observers.

Dutch poets often have this same compelling faculty of observation and a lyrical bent that results from seeing and finding it difficult to vent one's feelings extemporaneously. They are full of the mystery of their shrouded polders and lakes, the mobile skies above them and the unpredictable sea with its promise of far away and exotic travel. There is also that strange incomparable light that sweeps across the sky and changes everything it touches into an object of poetry. It may come from the reflection of the ambient sea or from the sun being sifted through hundreds of millions of particles of water that veil the country, even on a hot summer day. Possibly both, but whatever the cause, it is unique. Sights to dream of and impossible to tell!

It is enlightening, by contrast, to see what a Dutch landscape looks like when viewed through foreign eyes. Claude Monet, the great French impressionist, visited Holland in 1871. The warm colours of his 'Windmills near Zaandam' have very little in common with the silvery grey tones used by the Dutch landscape artists of the period. During his second trip in 1886, the Frenchman also made a number of spectacular paintings of tulip fields. His painter's eye had been struck by the brightness of their colours. 'A riot of colour', wrote one critic disparagingly, while another saw it as 'vegetation seen by a hallucinating mind.'

Another French painter by the name of Amand Gauthier, came to Holland some years before Monet and simply refused to accept that Dutch painters were capable of correctly rendering the

'The typical Dutch landscape viewed through foreign eyes.'

Claude Monet (1840-1927), Windmills near Zaandam, oil on canvas, 1871, 47 x 73 cm.

light and colour of their homeland. He looked at Holland through other eyes and was apparently unable to see the many subtle changes in tone and colour resulting from that very special hazy filtered light. What Gauthier had been conditioned to see in France was harsher: blinding yellow light, red earth, mauve mountains and deep blue sea. In fact, that is what the Dutchman Vincent van Gogh was after when he moved to the south of France. As the art critic Robert Hughes put it: 'In such places, colour might take on a primary, clarified role. Far from the veils and nuances of Paris fog and Dutch rain, it would resolve itself into tonic declaration – nouns that stood for well-being. Such at least, was Van Gogh's hope.' How completely different was the visual experience of Dutch painters.

The members of the Hague School also went out into the countryside to paint. They knew the tulip fields, of course, but they were not inclined to paint such brash colours. The normal approach in Dutch landscape art was tonal painting in accordance with the tradition set by the great masters of the past.

Gerard Bilders – a promising young nineteenth century painter who died at an early age – once put it like this: 'I seek to find a tone which we call coloured grey; in other words, to reduce all colours, however bright they may be, to a single hue in order to create the impression of a warm and aromatic grey.' He went on to exclaim ecstatically: 'To preserve the mood of a grey in a bright green is extremely difficult and anyone who manages to do so may consider himself a happy mortal.'

Paul Joseph Constantin Gabriël (1828-1903), Landscape near Overschie, oil on canvas, 66 x 102 cm .

The variegated play of toned colours and the magic light of Holland are naturally conducive to a highly poetical sense of reality. Dutch art is permeated by what is referred to as 'stemmingskunst', the art of conveying an atmosphere or a mood. Leo van Heyningen's pastel and charcoal drawing is a perfect example of this 'stemmingskunst' and he continues the long tradition of lovingly rendering interiors, still-lifes, ordinary day-to-day scenes and using these motives to create a feeling of intimacy. He has chosen a corner in his study. Something he sees every day. The door is open as though he had forgotten to close it before he started drawing. So he has used it to frame the rather unexpected stuffed heron on his desk. There is something a bit old-fashioned about the plain pre-World War II furniture and this adds a touch of dreaminess to the picture.

And outdoors, just how lyrical and engrossed a painter can become when he tries to absorb the beauty of a Dutch river landscape is evidenced by one out of hundreds of attempts by Willem den Ouden to capture the fleeting light in a drawing.

Leo van Heijningen (1955), Interior with Heron, pastel/conté, ca. 1987, 55 x 40 cm.

Willem den Ouden (1928), Dike near Varik, drawing, 1990/91.

Perhaps to take the edge off their sensitivity, the Dutch lay claim to a very particular brand of common sense. It is called 'nuchterheid' and must not be ignored even when writing about painting. Foreigners may wonder why everybody in Holland keeps on insisting that they are 'nuchter' and turn to a dictionary to find out what the word means. They will find a number of definitions, including: not drunk; reasonable; sober-minded and businesslike. Clearly, the last of these must be retained. To remain 'nuchter' in all situations and under all circumstances is a cherished national virtue.

In painting, 'nuchterheid' is illustrated by a clear preference for simple and even humble subjects. Make-believe and exaggeration hold little appeal; moderation will always prevail. Although there was, for instance, a tendency towards pathos in the paintings of the nineteenth century romanticists, even they kept their sentimentality within reasonable bounds. 'Nuchterheid' also tends to reject stardom. Artists who have made significant and even revolutionary contributions to the international art scene – like Jongkind, Van Gogh, Karel Appel or Willem de Kooning – have often chosen to work abroad, where they apparently felt that they could more freely develop their exceptional talents. As for pomp and pretentiousness, the Dutch are sincerely and deeply allergic to any attempt at outward display.

There is a story about King Louis XIV of France walking into a room stacked with Dutch paintings taken as booty when his troops invaded Holland in 1672. After taking one look at them, he turned away in disgust, ordering that 'those maggots' be removed from his sight. For the 'Roi Soleil', the purpose of art could only be to create illusion – in his case to glorify – by formally recreating reality. The idea that art could be concerned with ordinary subjects and represent them as they were was totally foreign to his way of thinking.

Another interesting example is that of Jan Willem Pieneman who, at the beginning of the nineteenth century, undertook to paint the largest historical work ever made in Holland. It was supposed to commemorate the role of the Prince of Orange at the battle of Waterloo, but Pieneman failed miserably to dramatize the event. Not a single button was omitted on the uniforms nor a single feather on a headpiece, as pure Dutch 'nuchterheid' prevented him from exploiting the artifice of histrionics. Rearing horses with flaring nostrils, whirling swords and heroic poses would have brought the whole scene to life, but such drama was contrary to the accepted norms of the culture in which he lived, and no doubt also to his own presumably fastidious nature. It took him six years to finish the painting, two of which were required for the portrait studies of Wellington and his staff alone!

Left: Théodore Géricault (1791-1824), 'Officier de chasseurs à cheval de la garde impériale, chargeant', oil on canvas, 1812, 292 x 194 cm.

Middle: Jan Willem Pieneman (1779-1853), The Battle of Waterloo, oil on canvas, 1818/24, 5.76 x 8.36 cm.

Right: Gerard Ter Borch (1617-1681), Watering soldier on horseback, pen drawing, 1631, 9.2 x 6.0 cm.

There is more drum and trumpet in the representation of a single guard on horseback by the French nineteenth century painter Theodore Gericault than in the whole vast work by Pieneman. Perhaps, when all is said and done, 'nuchterheid' is really nothing else but getting people off their high horses? The urinating soldier on the sketch by Gerard ter Borch can't be bothered to do even that.

The twilight proposition seems a nice and appropriate way of letting the curtain fall on this book about the Dutch and the country they live in. Observers of human cultures have laid claim to a correlation between different types of sunrises and sunsets and the temperament of the inhabitants of the countries concerned. This unusual theory would have it that the northern sun stirs the soul whereas the southern sun appeals to the body.

The French poet Jules Tellier who espoused this theory once wrote that a northern sunrise was 'a struggle, a confused scrummage, an unwillingness of the shadowy spirits of the night to let go of darkness'. This, he felt, affected the psyche of the people who lived in these regions. The inhabitants of countries, on the other hand, where 'day comes immediately when summoned... and the sun rises resolutely can have nothing that is ambiguous and troubled'.

Left: Edvard Munch (1863-1944), The Scream, oil, 1893, 37 7/8" x 30 5/8 ".

Right: Henri Matisse (1869-1954), 'Luxe, calme et volupté' , oil on canvas, 1904-1905, 95 x 116 cm.

There is, indeed, a world of difference between the sensuous effects of form and colour under the bright Mediterranean sun so warmly depicted by the Frenchman, Matisse, in his painting, 'Luxe, calme et volupte', and, to take an example from the opposite extreme, the mental anguish portrayed in the angst-ridden pictures of Edvard Munch's like his world-famous painting 'The Scream', in which the tortured soul is set against the incandescent sky of Munch's native Norway. Geographically, the two scenes are latitudinally about 20 degrees apart. Holland is situated on the 52nd parallel: exactly in the middle.

According to this twilight theory, the prosaic and literal passage from day to night and from night to day in southern regions furthers the development of a clear, matter of fact mind, whereas the drawn-out and wavering sunrises and sunsets of the north are conducive to philosophical musing and metaphysical emotions. Dutch landscape painting in many ways falls under the northern romantic tradition with its heavy stress on a spiritual empathy with nature rather than on its physical enjoyment. 'I see in nature, for example in trees, expression and, as it were, a soul,' wrote Vincent van Gogh to his brother Theo.

However, it is not in keeping with the national character to make a display of deep personal feelings. The Dutch are a cautious people who do not easily open up. The slow descent of the sun in Mesdag's painting illuminates the broad expanse of the sky and the sea. The impression is of 'calm' but the qualifications of 'luxury' and 'sensuality' would hardly be suited to describe this sunset. It is rather something quiet and gradual, and reassuringly steady.

Hendrik Willem Mesdag (1831-1915), Summer Evening on Scheveningen Beach, canvas, 1897, 178 x 139 cm.

Neither the Dutch nor Dutch artists are a species apart with identical characteristics, or an industrial brand that turns out replica models. Many Dutch artists do not meet the descriptions and criteria given in this book and it would be extremely hard to distinguish their works from those of artists in other countries. Conversely, there are enough examples of painters outside Holland whose interests and approach to art are very similar to their Dutch counterparts.

Take Gherardo delle Notti, for one. He was none other than Gerard Honthorst, one of the Dutch seventeenth century Caravaggists, who was famous in Italy and in his homeland for his use of artificial lighting. His art is based on effect rather than on mood which is what his fellow painters generally try to render. The portraits of the celebrities of the day – clothed and unclothed – by the painter from Rotterdam – Kees van Dongen – made him one of the stars of Paris during the 'Belle Epoque'. His works are a delightful chromatic feast and quite

un-Dutch. Jan Sluijters, who spent some time in Paris at the turn of the century, also acquired a lightness of touch and vibrant colours, that for a long time made him suspect to his more serious-minded countrymen.

Many foreign artists, on the other hand, have worked in the way of the Dutch. It is said that on his death-bed English painter, John Crome's last words about the famous Dutch painter were : 'Hobbema! My dear Hobbema! How I have loved you...' He recommended to his students to study Ruisdael, Cuyp, Van der Neer, Van Goyen and other seventeenth century Dutch masters. Another Englishman, John Constable, called his London home 'Ruisdael House'. He was fascinated by skies; his many studies of clouds make him akin to a Weissenbruch, a Jan Voerman or a Gerard Wensma. And, was it not the well known French painter Camille Corot who once spoke about 'the little songs I sing up in my grey clouds?' He was acquainted with Theodore Rousseau, Millet, Diaz and Troyon

of the French Barbizon School just outside the forest of Fontainebleau. They like the Dutch, were masters of tonal painting.

Dutch painting as a whole, however, indubitably has a specificity that no one will deny. Moreover, the very profusion of those, who, from one century to another, have reverted to the medium of painting, is remarkable. Holland continues to be a country of painters; indeed their density per square kilometer must be one of the highest in the world.

Given that Holland has been conferred upon the distinction of being 'the kingdom of pictorial expression', how best can the phenomenon be explained? Perhaps the answer is very simple after all: the Dutch born American writer, Hendrik Willem van Loon, provides a valuable insight when he wrote: 'Indeed I would go so far as to say that the Low Countries are one of the few parts of the world where every window becomes the frame for a very definite and exceedingly paintable little landscape...'

'Indeed I would go so far as to say that the Low Countries are one of the few parts of the world where every window becomes the frame for a very definite and exceedingly paintable little landscape...'

LIST OF POEMS